SUPER-CHARGED
SMOOTHIES

SUPER-CHARGED
SMOOTHIES

More Than 60 Recipes
for Energizing Smoothies

BY *Mary Corpening Barber*
AND *Sara Corpening Whiteford,*
with nutritional information by
Alison Eastwood

PHOTOGRAPHS BY *Jenifer Altman*

CHRONICLE BOOKS
SAN FRANCISCO

Text copyright © 2010 by Mary Corpening
Barber and Sara Corpening Whiteford.
Photographs copyright © 2010 by
Jenifer Altman.
All rights reserved. No part of this book
may be reproduced in any form without
written permission from the publisher.

Library of Congress Cataloging-in-Publication
Data available.

ISBN 978-0-8118-7024-5

Manufactured in China.

Prop and food styling by Jenifer Altman.
Designed by Tracy Sunrize Johnson
Typesetting by Tracy Sunrize Johnson
The photographer wishes to thank Amy Gillett.

10 9 8 7 6 5 4 3 2 1

Chronicle Books LLC
680 Second Street
San Francisco, California 94107

www.chroniclebooks.com

THanKS!

TO DIANE MORGAN for inviting us to her *Grill Every Day* book signing where we serendipitously bumped into Peter Perez who instigated this project!

TO HALEY NOLDE, the glue and mortar of this project, for helping us shape the text of this book. Your research added immensely to the project, not to mention your finesse of words and your magical ability to consolidate our thoughts. Your collaborative efforts tightened the lid on this blender project and for that we are greatly appreciative.

TO ALISON HORTON EASTWOOD for helping us piece together the nutritional component. Your level of professionalism is unparalleled, and we could never have completed this project without all your sound advice. We've all come a long way since *Super Smoothies!*

TO JEFFERY ADLER, who hired us as the product development team for Dlush, a youth-beverage joint based in San Diego. The inspiration from Dlush has affected this project in more ways than we can count. Creativity spawns in many ways, and loads of it poured out of the Dlush test kitchen.

TO CHAYA RYVKA DIEHL and the pioneers of Café Gratitude for opening our eyes to the glory of raw food preparation. Incorporating more raw foods into our diet has enlightened us and fueled our smoothie repertoire.

TO LILA STEINLE, DELI HAYNES, LUCY BOWEN, and **STEPHANIE SCHREIBER** for embracing our Smoothie Revival Program (featured online at www.maryandsara.com) and helping us flesh out the details.

TO BILL LEBLOND, our steadfast editor at Chronicle Books and to **DOE COOVER,** our crafty agent, who brought this concept into fruition.

TO THE WONDERFUL TEAM AT CHRONICLE BOOKS, who made this book a reality: **CARRIE BRADLEY** for her super-sharp copyediting ability, **SARAH BILLINGSLEY** for her wonderful editorial assistance, **JENIFER ALTMAN** for her fabulous photography, and **TRACY JOHNSON** for her cutting-edge design.

TO JACK and ERIK, our smoothie enthusiast husbands, for their unwavering support; and to our kiddos, **JACKSON, WILLIAM, JOHN, LUCY, and ELLA,** for their insightful and always truthful feedback. Our self-proclaimed smoothie aficionados have molded our decision making along the way.

WE COLLECTIVELY THANK EVERYBODY, once again, for bringing *Super charged Smoothies* to life! We feel charged by all these exciting recipes and hope you do too!

CONTENTS

INTRODUCTION

WE ARE DELIGHTED to introduce our latest smoothie collection. After completing a wealth of new combinations, our passion for health and vitality has exploded. We feel better than ever: more alkaline, more hydrated, more energetic, more vibrant, and more alive! We urge you to try this new wave of smoothies brimming with superfoods and all their nutrients.

WHAT EXCITES US THE MOST about writing recipes is discovering new, healthful food products and turning other people on to them. This groundbreaking smoothie book is an introduction to a wide variety of superfoods, ranging from acai to goji berries, pomegranate juice to probiotic Greek yogurt, and agave nectar to coconut butter. Get to know Thai young coconuts, chia seeds, yacon syrup, cacao powder, and much, much more. If you can't find these exciting new-age ingredients at your local health-food store, they are all at your fingertips with a few clicks on your computer.

WE REMEMBER THE EXCITEMENT that we felt when we created Cacao Frenzy, an unforgettable chocolate milk made with cacao powder, raw hazelnuts, and Medjool dates that is packed with protein and antioxidants. Without an ounce of refined sugar, it's decadent, healthful, and energizing, too! Who would have thought that matcha powder, the innermost part of the green tea leaf, could be so compatible with jasmine tea, frozen grapes, and avocado? Yes, avocado! Or that raw cashews could turn a blueberry smoothie into a creamy protein shake beloved by kids?

That breakthrough was revolutionary to us, and before we knew it, we were blending all sorts of nuts in shakes. Then there was the thrill of Sara's daughter Lucy falling in love with Raspberry Ritual, our cottage cheese and raspberry kefir blend—a brilliant blast of calcium and probiotic power for a kid who does not even like milk!

WE KNEW WE WERE ONTO SOMETHING BIG when our dear mom from North Carolina, who is skeptical of our California ways, fell in love with our Essential Greens chapter. Even she embraced the concept of making RAW ORGANIC vegetable smoothies and found she particularly fancied our Apple, Cuke, Parsley, Mint medley. If you like the sound of these powerful foods or already have them in your habits, you're the perfect candidate for our super-charged Smoothie Revival Program. Check out our Web site at www.maryandsara.com for a seven-day detail of healthful eating with myriad benefits, from weight loss to a good night's sleep—one day at a time, you will be rewarded, renewed, and revitalized.

AS WE ALL KNOW, smoothies can be sweet-tooth satisfiers, energy enhancers, cleansing on-the-go meal replacements, pick-me-up snacks, terrific kid-pleasing shakes, and even alka-linizing toddies for adults. What a great way to consume a variety of vitamins and other healthful ingredients. Super-charged smoothies will increase your antioxidant intake, strengthen your immune system, slenderize, alkalinize, and energize. With the push of a button, you can whirr your way to a healthier, super-charged lifestyle.

ENJOY!

OUR SUPER-CHARGED SUPERFOODS PANTRY

We encourage you to get to know these nutrient-dense super-foods and make them a part of your life. Whether their claims to nutrition fame lie in a richness of vitamins, minerals, anti-oxidants, essential fatty acids, or probiotics, these foods are natural, live, and minimally processed. All of these ingredients can be found at Whole Foods, your local natural-foods store, or online. See Binders and Other Key Ingredients (page 122) for nutritional benefits, brands, and Web sites that we like, and more information on this dynamic dozen.

1. **Acai**
2. **Cacao powder and nibs**
3. **Chia seeds**
4. **Flaxseed/flaxseed oil**
5. **Goji berries**
6. **Kefir, Greek yogurt, and other probiotic drinks**
7. **Matcha powder**
8. **Pomegranate juice**
9. **Raw nuts, nut butters, and seeds**
10. **Thai young coconuts**
11. **Hemp seeds**
12. **Sprouted live organic granola**

THE SCOOP ON BLENDERS

We would be remiss if we didn't share with you our addiction to our high-speed blender. We simply could not live without it. High-speed blenders, such as the Vita-Mix, are versatile appliances that are well worth their higher cost. They are fantastic for smoothies but can do much more. The Vita-Mix has a powerful 2-horsepower (1,380-watt) motor; its blades spin so fast that you can chop all of the ingredients for a soup in just a few minutes. The motor is also powerful enough to make perfectly blended melted cheese fondues and to grind grains into flour! We particularly love high-speed blenders for their 64-oz (2-L) jar (perfect for making nut milks), but note that polycarbonate can scratch and stain over time. Be prepared . . . a high-speed blender sounds like a jet engine, but the power it generates is unparalleled, and the long-term durability makes it worth the investment.

By no means do you have to have a fancy, expensive blender to make smoothies, but we do recommend a blender with sharp blades and a strong motor. Even if you have an old blender with a dull blade and a wimpy motor, you can still make smoothies; just adjust the recipes, if necessary. You may cut the fruit into smaller pieces, for example, or add more liquid and less ice. If the food packs around the blade, you may also have to sneak peeks more frequently, use a spatula to dislodge the food, and then reblend.

CHAPTER 1

ENERGIZING ENHANCERS

IT'S NO SECRET THAT AMERICANS LOVE FEELING SUPER-CHARGED.

People seek the big energy buzz, but not everyone wants the sugar, the caffeine, and all the other chemically produced stimulants that fortify many of the energy drinks on the market today. This chapter is full of smoothies containing power foods that increase energy and health. They give you a lift, they are pure and natural, and they taste fantastic. If you are looking for a tasty, energizing treat, whip out your blender and celebrate this new wave of smoothies.

We savor **CASHEW BLUE** in the morning for its protein-packed deliciousness. **GREEN ENERGY** makes for a wholesome lunch that'll give you a dose of energy between carpools or meetings. If you prefer spice in your life, try our **CHA CHA CHAI** for a fiber-filled variation of an iced chai latte. **BANANA-HAZELNUT JOE** is fantastic for anyone who's looking for a healthful alternative to the afternoon cookie-coffee fix, and **KOMBUCHA, BABY!** is a juicy, fruity energy blend with no crash-and-burn effect—perfect for pre- or post-workout. Just pick your potion. Each recipe delivers an energy-enhancing effect.

CaSHeW BLUe

Sara whirled up this unexpected combination of blueberries and cashews in a desperate attempt to incorporate protein into her daughter Lucy's diet. No fan of meat, Lucy adores this delicious protein-powered, antioxidant-rich blend. The mildly flavored cashews are nearly undetectable, but they add a subtle richness and brilliance to this shake. A bonus for those on the other end of the age spectrum: blueberries have been shown not only to halt the aging process, but to actually reverse it.

MAKES ABOUT 2 1/2 CUPS/600 ML; SERVES 2

1 1/2 cups/360 ml **fresh-pressed apple juice**
1/2 cup/55 g **raw cashews, preferably soaked and drained** (SEE PAGE 124)
1 1/2 cups/170 g **frozen blueberries**
1/4 tsp **vanilla extract/essence**
Maple syrup (optional)

Combine the apple juice, cashews, blueberries, and vanilla in the blender. Blend until smooth. Sweeten with maple syrup, if desired.

cacao Frenzy

When you are looking for a little "something something" as a late-afternoon pick-me-up, this frothy cacao frappé is your ticket to revival. Cacao, the source for all chocolate and cocoa products, contains chemicals that enhance physical and mental well-being. Not only does the cacao give you a zing, the hazelnuts and coconut butter add a dose of protein that is sure to energize. Although expensive and somewhat hard to find, coconut butter is a divine addition for the coconut lover, but this smoothie is delish with or without. Although store-bought almond milk works fine, for this mix, we enthusiastically recommend making your own (see page 122).

MAKES ABOUT 2 1/2 CUPS/600 ML; SERVES 2

1 1/4 cups/300 ml **almond milk OR milk**

3 or 4 **Medjool dates, pits removed**

2 to 3 tbsp **raw cacao powder**

1 tbsp **raw organic coconut butter OR coconut oil (optional)**

2 tsp **vanilla extract/essence**

1/4 cup/30 g **raw hazelnuts OR almonds, preferably soaked and drained** (SEE PAGE 122)

8 to 10 **ice cubes**

Combine 1/2 cup/120 ml of the milk, the dates, cacao powder, coconut butter (if using), vanilla, and nuts in a blender. Blend until smooth. Add the remaining 3/4 cup/180 ml milk and the ice. Blend until frothy.

peach pie maté

We have acquired a taste for yerba maté, a traditional South American infusion with an herbal, grassy essence. If you find its smoky tobacco flavor off-putting at first, you may well change your mind when you sip this spicy peach delight. Maté is often marketed as a caffeine-free alternative to coffee and tea. Its chemical components are similar to those found in green tea, but yerba maté is more nutritious. Researchers at the Pasteur Institute and the Paris Scientific Society concluded that "it is difficult to find a plant in any area of the world equal to maté in nutritional value" and that yerba maté contains "practically all of the vitamins necessary to sustain life." One cup and you will no doubt feel more alert, focused, and energized—without the jitters.

MAKES ABOUT 2 1/2 CUPS/600 ML; SERVES 2

1 1/2 cups/255 g **frozen peaches**
1 cup/240 ml **strong-brewed yerba maté, chilled**
3/4 cup/170 g **vanilla soy frozen yogurt**
1/2 cup/120 ml **passion-fruit juice**
1/2 tsp **ground cinnamon**
1/8 tsp **freshly grated nutmeg**

Combine the peaches, yerba maté, soy frozen yogurt, passion-fruit juice, cinnamon, and nutmeg in a blender. Blend until smooth.

Banana-Hazelnut Joe

Hazelnuts, coffee, and vanilla collide harmoniously in a delectable coffee smoothie. Though this sensation can be blended with standard home-brewed java, one of the secrets of its smoothness lies in the cold-brew technique. The other is in the hazelnuts. Not only do these healthful nuggets lend a unique indulgence to the overall flavor, they also contain a rich source of nutrients that protect the heart. Never has a cup of joe been so heart-healthy!

MAKES ABOUT 2 1/2 CUPS/600 ML; SERVES 2

3/4 cup/180 ml **hazelnut milk (PAGE 127)**
1/2 cup/120 ml **cold-brew coffee (SEE NOTE),
   strong-brewed coffee, OR espresso, chilled**
1 **frozen banana, sliced**
3/4 cup/170 g **low-fat vanilla frozen yogurt**
1/4 cup/30 g **raw hazelnuts, preferably soaked
   and drained**
3 or 4 **ice cubes**
2 tsp **raw cacao powder or unsweetened
   cocoa powder**
2 tsp **vanilla extract/essence**
Pinch of **ground cinnamon**

Combine the hazelnut milk, coffee, and banana in a blender. Add the frozen yogurt, hazelnuts, ice, cacao powder, vanilla, and cinnamon. Blend until smooth.

NOTE: The cold-water brewing process extracts the natural, delicious flavors of coffee while leaving behind undesirable bitter acids and oils. For ordering information, go to www.toddycafe.com. We like their ice coffee blend.

GREEN ENERGY

This smoothie is the green energy alternative to a milkshake made with green tea ice cream. You simply won't believe that this dairy-free, antioxidant-charged concoction is so rich and creamy. Because matcha increases energy and improves mental alertness, slug this before a workout or in the afternoon during that four o'clock lull. For that matter, why not surprise your evening guests with an unexpected glass of Green Energy after some take-out sushi? You may feel frisky well into the night!

MAKES ABOUT 2 1/2 CUPS/600 ML; SERVES 2

2 tbsp **raw honey,** plus more to taste
1 cup/240 ml **warm strong-brewed jasmine tea**
3/4 cup/105 g **chopped ripe avocado**
1 cup/170 g **frozen green grapes**
3/4 cup/180 ml **vanilla soy milk, made into ice cubes**
1/2 tsp **matcha powder**

Dissolve the 2 tbsp honey in the warm tea. Taste and add more honey, if you like. Refrigerate until chilled. Combine the sweetened tea, avocado, grapes, soy-milk ice cubes, and matcha powder in a blender. Blend until smooth.

FACTOID: Did you know that matcha boosts the metabolic rate by 35 to 40 percent?

THAI BUBBLE TEA SLUSH

We first discovered Thai tea with boba (a.k.a. Thai bubble tea) on Clement Street in San Francisco while doing research for Dlush, a youth beverage hotspot in Southern California. Thai tea is a black tea traditionally made with condensed milk, sugar, and cream. The earthy, smoky Thai tea jives well with the pear, and the novel tapioca balls give a real bounce to the slush. We encourage you to try quick-cooking boba, which cooks in 5 minutes—or if you want to go boba-less, this Thai slush stands tall on its own.

MAKES ABOUT 2 1/2 CUPS/600 ML; SERVES 2

1/2 cup/120 ml **fresh-pressed apple juice**

1 1/2 cups/255 g **peeled and diced pears, preferably Comice**

3 tbsp **condensed milk,** plus more to taste

3 tbsp **half-and-half/half cream**

1 cup/240 ml **strong-brewed Thai tea** (SEE NOTE), **made into ice cubes**

1 cup/220 g **cooked boba, cooled to room temperature** (SEE NOTE)

Combine the apple juice, pears, 3 tbsp condensed milk, and half-and-half/half cream in a blender. Add the tea ice cubes and blend until smooth. Taste and add more condensed milk, if you like. Put half of the boba in the bottom of each of two glasses and pour the smoothie on top, dividing it evenly.

Serve with a spoon or a fat straw.

NOTE: High-quality Thai tea and quick-cooking boba can be ordered online at www.bobateadirect.com. Follow the package instructions for cooking boba; 1 cup/155 g express boba yields 1 cup/220 g cooked. We strain the cooked pearls and stir in 1 tsp raw honey and a pinch of sea salt.

KOMBUCHA, BABY!

The Barber and Whiteford households are huge fans of kombucha (pronounced KOM-BOO-CHA), which we affectionately call kom-boooch! This effervescent probiotic elixir is a tad vinegary, so we drink it more for the way it makes us feel than for its taste. At the onset of the flu a few years ago, Sara discovered kombucha at a natural-foods store in San Francisco's famed Haight-Ashbury district, and she experienced a miraculous and unforgettable turnaround. It may not always cure your flu, but kombucha has myriad health claims, from supporting alkalinity to detoxifying the body, and it provides an energizing lift every time you drink it. Long live kom-boooch, baby!

MAKES ABOUT 2 1/2 CUPS/600 ML; SERVES 2

1 cup/240 ml **grape kombucha, such as Synergy**
1 **fresh ripe banana**
1 cup/115 g **frozen strawberries**
3/4 cup/85 g **frozen blueberries**

Combine the kombucha and banana in a blender. Add the strawberries and blueberries and blend until smooth.

POMEGRANATE MOCHA

Celebrate the addictive nature of this smoothie! Brimming with antioxidants, isoflavones, and fiber, this jet fuel of a blend boosts health and energy, all the while enhancing your mood. Pomegranate juice contains high levels of antioxidants, even more than red wine and green tea. Still more astounding is that the cacao, which is raw chocolate powder, has twenty times more antioxidants than red wine and thirty times more than green tea. Tip this back before a workout for a healthful Red Bull effect.

MAKES ABOUT 2 1/2 CUPS/600 ML; SERVES 2

1 cup/240 ml **vanilla soy milk**
1/2 cup/120 ml **cold-brew coffee** (SEE NOTE, PAGE 17), **strong-brewed coffee, OR espresso, chilled**
1 cup/115 g **frozen strawberries**
3/4 cup/180 ml **pomegranate juice, made into ice cubes**
3 tbsp **agave nectar**
2 tbsp **raw cacao powder or unsweetened cocoa powder**

Combine the soy milk, coffee, strawberries, pomegranate ice cubes, agave nectar, and cacao powder in a blender. Blend until smooth.

CHa CHa CHai

With its soft-butter consistency and musky undertones, it is no wonder that Christopher Columbus reputedly called papaya the "fruit of the angels." Here it melds beautifully with the wholesome glory of nectarines, spiced black tea, ginger, and raw honey. Cha Cha Chai is as yummy to drink as it is fun to say and has great health benefits, too. The vitamin C in the nectarines and papaya is a powerful antioxidant and anti-inflammatory agent, which may decrease the incidence of asthma symptoms. A large preliminary study has shown that young children with asthma experience significantly less wheezing if they eat a diet high in fruits rich in vitamin C. Also, both fruits are a good source of fiber, which is known to lower cholesterol levels. Raw honey, which is not heated or filtered, has an exceptionally high enzyme count that supports a healthy digestive system. Long-term effects of downing this gift from the bees may also give you a strong immune system.

MAKES ABOUT 2 1/2 CUPS/600 ML; SERVES 2

2 tbsp **raw honey, such as orange blossom**
3/4 cup/180 ml **warm strong-brewed chai tea**
1 1/2 cups/255 g **diced nectarines**
3/4 cup/130 g **diced fresh papaya, frozen**
1/2 tsp **peeled and chopped fresh ginger**
2 to 4 **ice cubes**

Dissolve the honey in the warm chai tea. Refrigerate until chilled. Combine the sweetened chai tea, nectarines, papaya, ginger, and ice in a blender. Blend until smooth.

FACTOID: Papaya contains the digestive enzyme *papain*, which is used like bromelain, a similar enzyme found in pineapple, to treat sports injuries, other causes of trauma, and allergies.

CHAPTER 2

WELLNESS BLENDS

FOOD AS MEDICINE IS OUR MANTRA.

There is no denying the health benefits of fresh, raw, organic fruits and veggies. The truth is that fruits and vegetables improve immune function to ward off disease and other ailments. Although we can't promise cures, this chapter includes a host of ingredients that contribute to vitality and wellness. Whether you need to nourish your female system, fight a cold, battle cancer, or stave off arthritis, we have a smoothie for you.

Packed with more natural vitamin C than any other food source on the planet, our camu camu-fortified **SUPER C** smoothie is a great cold buster. If you are looking to ease the effects of menopause with the power of soy, indulge in **HUSH THE HORMONES.** Feeling sick to your stomach? Swig **NO MORE NAUSEA.** And if you just can't seem to remember anything these days, try our majestic blue BLUEBERRY BRAIN BOOST. Who knew that blueberries may improve cognitive function? *Maybe you just forgot!*

SUPER C

What better way to stave off a cold or flu than to double down on vitamin C! We encourage you to get to know camu camu, which has more natural vitamin C than any other food on planet Earth (find out more on page 124). This super-tart superfood contains thirty to sixty times more vitamin C than an orange. We order this tart orange powder from Navitas Naturals, but a readily available vitamin package, such Emergen-C, makes a fine substitute. Be it camu camu or Emergen-C, down this mega C flu-busting blend and put your tissues away.

MAKES ABOUT 2 1/2 CUPS/600 ML; SERVES 2

1/2 cup/120 ml **fresh orange juice**
1/2 cup/120 ml **filtered water**
2 tsp **camu camu powder**
3/4 cup/130 g **chopped fresh mango**
1 cup/115 g **frozen strawberries**
1 **frozen banana, sliced**

Combine the orange juice, water, and camu camu powder in a blender. Add the mango, strawberries, and banana. Blend until smooth.

NOTE: If you don't have a perfectly ripe mango on hand, frozen mango works well as a substitute. Use a fresh ripe banana instead of a frozen one if using frozen mango.

Happy Heart

Did you know that heart disease is the leading cause of death in the United States? You will make your heart happy every time you swig this purple delight. The mixed berries contain a concentration of heart-healthy antioxidants and the creamy addition of soy milk provides both isoflavones and soy protein, both of which have been shown to improve cholesterol levels, thus helping to lower heart disease risk. Down this true blue, and you'll feel better in a heartbeat.

MAKES ABOUT 2 1/2 CUPS/600 ML; SERVES 2

3/4 cup/180 ml **blueberry juice**
1/2 cup/120 ml **vanilla soy milk**
1 **fresh ripe banana**
2 cups/225 g **frozen mixed berries**

Combine the blueberry juice, soy milk, and banana in a blender. Add the mixed berries. Blend until smooth.

HUSH THE HORMONES

Hush your hunger cravings by downing this luscious cherry-banana beverage and you may hush your hormones, too. Incorporating soy-based foods in your diet is a great way to increase your isoflavone intake, which may ease symptoms of menopause. Soy consumption has other benefits as well, including protection against heart disease, certain cancers, and osteoporosis.

MAKES ABOUT 2 1/2 CUPS/600 ML; SERVES 2

3/4 cup/180 ml **pomegranate-apple juice**
3/4 cup/170 g **low-fat cherry soy yogurt**
3/4 cup/85 g **frozen cherries**
1 **frozen banana**
4 to 6 **ice cubes**

Combine the pomegranate-apple juice and soy yogurt in a blender. Add the cherries, banana, and ice. Blend until smooth.

NO MORE Nausea

Whether it's a flu bug, morning sickness, chemotherapy, or motion sickness, nausea really is the pits! We added a healthy dose of fresh ginger to this wholesome peachy purée to soothe the intestinal tract. Ginger has long been known for its healing powers. King Henry VIII of England even used it to protect against the plague. Though we may not give ginger as much credit as Henry, we do know that it will ease a basic bout of nausea. Suffer no more!

MAKES ABOUT 2 1/2 CUPS/600 ML; SERVES 2

3/4 cup/170 g **low-fat apricot-mango yogurt**
3/4 cup/180 ml **apricot nectar, chilled**
1 1/2 cups/255 g **frozen diced peaches**
1 tsp **fresh lemon juice**
3/4 tsp **peeled and chopped fresh ginger**
3 to 5 **ice cubes**

Combine the yogurt and apricot nectar in a blender. Add the peaches, lemon juice, ginger, and ice. Blend until smooth.

cancer KICKER

We urge you to be open-minded when it comes to savory smoothies. This wholesome gazpacho blend is oh-so-satisfying, and we drink it all year 'round. The subtle nutty flavor and smooth, buttery texture of the avocado blend beautifully with the crunchy, hydrating cukes. The avocados are rich in oleic acid, which can reduce blood pressure and help fend off cancer. And attention, men: he who consumes ten or more servings per week of lycopene-containing tomato products has a dramatically reduced risk of prostate cancer. Think of this antioxidant-rich blend as medicine that never tasted so good.

MAKES ABOUT 2 1/2 CUPS/600 ML; SERVES 2

---

1 1/2 cups/360 ml **tomato juice, chilled**
1/3 cup/75 g **low-fat lemon yogurt**
1/4 cup/20 g **chopped green/spring onions, white and tender green parts**
4 **medium fresh basil leaves**
1 tbsp **fresh lemon juice**
1/4 tsp **sea salt,** plus more to taste
Freshly ground pepper
1 cup/140 g **chopped ripe avocado**
3/4 cup/105 g **roughly chopped organic OR English/hothouse cucumber (seeded and peeled if necessary)**

Combine the tomato juice and yogurt in a blender. Add the green/spring onion, basil, lemon juice, 1/4 tsp salt, and pepper to taste. Blend until smooth. Add the avocado and cucumber and pulse a few times, just until incorporated but still chunky. Do not overblend. Taste and adjust the seasoning with salt and pepper.

PREGO Mama

Beetroots give this smoothie a fabulously rich fuchsia color. A perfect pink bouquet of vitality, it tastes as vibrant as it looks. Not only are beetroots rich in folic acid, they are also rich in antioxidants, as are goji berries. During pregnancy, it is more important than ever to consume foods that are high in antioxidants to boost your immune system, and your growing babe's, too.

MAKES ABOUT 2 1/2 CUPS/600 ML; SERVES 2

1 1/4 cups/300 ml **passion-fruit juice**
1/3 cup/50 g **grated raw beets/beetroots**
1 cup/170 g **chopped frozen pineapple**
1 cup/170 g **chopped frozen mango**
1 tbsp **goji berries**
10 **medium fresh mint leaves**

Combine the passion-fruit juice, beets/beetroots, pineapple, and mango in a blender. Add the goji berries and mint. Blend until smooth.

NOTE: Folate is necessary for the production and maintenance of new cells. This is especially important during periods of rapid cell division and growth during pregnancy.

BLUEBERRY BRAIN BOOST

Recent studies show that the powerful antioxidants and phyto-chemicals in blueberries may improve cognitive function. Paired with walnuts, they make a blueberry smoothie that tops the antioxidant chart. The rich nuttiness of the walnuts complements the berries, and they may work a little magic on your memory. Word has it that walnuts contain essential fatty acids that support the development of brain cells and neurotransmitters, so sip this unforgettable smoothie and you may just forget less!

MAKES ABOUT 2 1/2 CUPS/600 ML; SERVES 2

1 cup/240 ml **fresh-pressed apple juice**
1 **fresh ripe banana**
1 1/2 cups/170 g **frozen blueberries**
1/2 cup/55 g **frozen raspberries**
1/4 cup/30 g **raw walnuts, preferably soaked and drained**

Combine the apple juice and banana in a blender. Add the blueberries, raspberries, and walnuts. Blend until smooth.

ADIOS, ARTHRITIS

If you are one of millions of people plagued by the debilitating effects of joint pain, do yourself a favor and consume more ginger. This spicy and pungent aromatic root contains potent anti-inflammatory compounds called gingerols. Regular consumption of these compounds is believed to have brought less pain and greater mobility to many people with osteoarthritis and rheumatoid arthritis. Be proactive and say adios to arthritis.

MAKES ABOUT 2 1/2 CUPS/600 ML; SERVES 2

1 1/2 cups/360 ml **vanilla kefir or probiotic vanilla drink, such as DanActive**
1 1/2 cups/255 g **chopped mango**
1 tsp **peeled and chopped fresh ginger**
Agave nectar
Pinch of **ground cardamom (optional)**

Combine the kefir, mango, ginger, agave nectar to taste, and cardamom (if using) in a blender. Blend until smooth.

PRETTY 'N' PINK

Raspberry-leaf tea is chock-full of vitamins and minerals, such as vitamin C and calcium. It contains an alkaloid called fragine, which strengthens the pelvic and uterine muscles and is thought to aid in healthy menstruation. Native Americans have used this herbal tonic for thousands of years to tone the female reproductive system. One sip of this oh-so-pink elixir and you may embrace Jackie Kennedy's prized words, "Above all else, I am a woman."

MAKES ABOUT 2 1/2 CUPS/600 ML; SERVES 2

2 tbsp **raw honey, such as orange blossom**
1 cup/240 ml **strong-brewed raspberry-leaf tea**
1 cup/115 g **fresh raspberries**
1 cup/240 ml **fresh-pressed apple juice, made into ice cubes**
1/4 cup/40 g **Incan berries (optional;** SEE NOTE)

Dissolve the honey in the warm tea. Refrigerate until chilled. Combine the sweetened tea, raspberries, apple-juice ice cubes, and Incan berries (if using) in a blender. Blend until smooth.

NOTE: Sun-dried Incan berries (also known as goldenberries or cape gooseberries) are sweet and tart "exotic" raisins that are high in protein for a fruit and will add a handful of health to this smoothie. The berries possess antiviral, anticarcinogenic, anti-inflammatory, antihistamine, and antioxidant properties.

CHAPTER 3

ANTIOXIDANTS ALL THE WAY

Oxidation, the combination of a substance with oxygen, can create atoms or groups of atoms called "free radicals" by leaving them with unpaired (an odd number of) electrons. These free radicals in turn cause cell damage in the body. Antioxidants are molecules that slow or prevent the oxidation of other molecules.

IF WE INCREASE OUR INTAKE OF ANTIOXIDANTS, WE STRENGTHEN OUR IMMUNE SYSTEM, WHICH HELPS PREVENT ILLNESS AND DELAYS THE PROCESS OF AGING.

The smoothies in this chapter are simply brimming with antioxidant-rich new-age ingredients such as pomegranate juice, goji berries, and Thai young coconuts—not to mention nutrient-dense staples like carrot juice, cherry tomatoes, and fresh raw nuts. Introduce yourself to a voluptuous **POM ACAI** smoothie for a satisfying megadose of antioxidants, or down a GOJI GREATNESS if you want to feel great! Embrace the unlikely, yet magnificent AVO-COLADA because, quite simply, it may make you feel young again.

Pom Acai

If you haven't yet discovered acai (pronounced ah-sigh-ee), make this smoothie and you might just become an acai ADDICT! *This exotic purple berry, loaded with vitamins, minerals, and antioxidants, comes from the Brazilian rain forest and is thought by many to be the world's best superfruit. Reminiscent of blackberries and blueberries, sweet acai comes alive when paired with teasingly tart, antioxidant-rich pomegranate juice. Keep your eye out for acai juice blends, as well as smoothie packs, which have less sugar and are found in the freezer section at natural-foods stores. Our kids love to top this smoothie with organic sprouted granola for a super-charged breakfast.*

MAKES ABOUT 2 1/2 CUPS/600 ML; SERVES 2

1 cup/240 ml **pomegranate juice**
1 **fresh ripe banana**
1 1/4 cups/140 g **frozen blueberries**
One 3 1/2-oz/100-g **frozen acai smoothie pack OR**
   1 cup/225 g **acai sorbet**

Combine the pomegranate juice and banana in a blender. Add the blueberries and acai. Blend until smooth.

GOJI GREATNESS

Goji berries may look like shriveled red raisins and taste a tad seedy on their own, but blended in this smoothie, the little berries transform into goji greatness. Used for some six thousand years by herbalists in China, Tibet, and India, this dried berry is loaded with antioxidants. Truly a wonder fruit, goji berries are thought to improve eyesight, protect the liver, promote longevity, and boost the immune system. Om, meet yum!

MAKES ABOUT 2 1/2 CUPS/600 ML; SERVES 2

1 cup/240 ml **goji juice or apple juice**
1 3/4 cups/200 g **frozen strawberries**
1/2 cup/115 g **passion-fruit sorbet**
2 tbsp **goji berries**

Combine the goji juice, strawberries, and sorbet in a blender. Blend until smooth. Add the goji berries and pulse until well incorporated.

COCONUT AMBROSIA

Both of us are coconut fanatics, so, needless to say, we have a huge crush on this ambrosia blend. The perfect start to any day, this room-temperature smoothie blend is chunky, a bit crunchy, and should be served with a spoon. Because our kids prefer smoothies with a milk-shake consistency, we had to coax them into this one. Now our little coconut lovers request this unexpected smoothie for breakfast.

If you are doing the Smoothie Revival Program (for more information see www.maryandsara.com), substitute 1 cup/240 ml canned coconut water (also labeled coconut juice) for the coconut milk, and add 1/4 cup/55 g more diced green apple and 2 tbsp whey protein for creaminess. Coconut water is an isotonic beverage that is a wonderful source of electrolytes.

MAKES ABOUT 2 1/2 CUPS/600 ML; SERVES 2

1 1/2 cups/360 ml **coconut milk, blended from water and meat of 1 Thai young coconut** (SEE NOTE)

1 or 2 **Medjool dates, pits removed**

1/2 tsp **vanilla extract/essence**

Pinch of **sea salt**

1 cup/115 g **fresh strawberries**

3/4 cup/85 g **diced green apple**

1/4 cup/30 g **raw almonds, preferably soaked and drained** (SEE PAGE 122)

Combine the coconut milk, dates, vanilla, and salt in a blender. Blend until smooth. Add the strawberries, apple, and almonds and pulse a few times, just until incorporated but still chunky. Do not overblend. Serve with a spoon.

NOTE: If Thai young coconut is unavailable, substitute a mixture of 2 parts canned coconut milk and 1 part filtered water for the homemade coconut milk.

AVO-COLADA

This virgin rendition of the famed piña colada is for pineapple and coconut lovers who are disenchanted with all the overly sweet, artificial concoctions out there. Avocado lends this wholesome blend an unparalleled creaminess without any dairy. The latest studies show that avocados can actually help lower cholesterol. To all those coconut devotees, knock back this indulgent colada without an ounce of guilt.

MAKES ABOUT 2 1/2 CUPS/600 ML; SERVES 2

1 1/4 cups/300 ml **coconut milk, blended from water and meat of 1 Thai young coconut** (SEE NOTE, FACING PAGE)

1/2 cup/70 g **chopped ripe avocado**

1 cup/170 g **frozen white grapes**

3/4 cup/130 g **chopped frozen pineapple**

1 tbsp plus 1 tsp **fresh lime juice**

1 tbsp **agave nectar**

Pinch of **sea salt**

2 **ice cubes**

Combine the coconut milk, avocado, grapes, pineapple, lime juice, agave nectar, salt, and ice in a blender. Blend until smooth.

FACTOID: Coconut water is a universal donor—it has the same electrolyte balance as human blood plasma. Coconut water has saved lives in third world countries through intravenous use.

Beta-Carotene Blast

You may remember your mother telling you that eating carrots was good for your eyes. It wasn't just an old wives' tale; carrots contain carotenoids, including beta-carotene and lutein, which may slow the progression of cataracts and prevent macular degeneration. High-carotenoid foods, especially the now famous beta-carotene, provide a source of vitamin A, lower risks for certain cancers and heart disease, boost immunity, and may even decrease infertility. So be good and drink your carrots!

MAKES ABOUT 2 1/2 CUPS/600 ML; SERVES 2

1/2 cup/120 ml **fresh-pressed carrot juice**
1/2 cup/120 ml **fresh orange juice** OR
  mangosteen nectar
1/2 **fresh ripe banana**
1 cup/170 g **chopped frozen peaches**
1 cup/170 g **chopped frozen pineapple**

Combine the carrot juice, orange juice, and banana in a blender. Add the peaches and pineapple. Blend until smooth.

Cran-Tastic

This cleansing concoction was inspired by our treasured cranberry-orange relish recipe, a staple at our Thanksgiving table. Amazingly delicious, this autumnal cranberry blend also deserves to be celebrated for its powerful health benefits. There are compounds in cranberries that help prevent urinary tract infections and play a role in resisting cancer. Cranberries also promote gastrointestinal and oral health. Some recent studies have revealed that cranberries are phytochemical powerhouses packed with five times the antioxidant content of broccoli. This cran-tastic blend will undoubtedly be a fantastic boost to your immune system.

MAKES ABOUT 2 1/2 CUPS/600 ML; SERVES 2

1 1/4 cups/300 ml **fresh-pressed apple juice**
3/4 cup/130 g **chopped frozen pineapple**
1/2 cup/55 g **frozen raspberries**
1/2 cup/55 g **frozen cranberries**
1/4 cup/30 g **raw pecans (optional)**
2 tbsp **agave nectar**
1/4 tsp **grated orange zest**
2 or 3 **ice cubes**

Combine the apple juice, pineapple, raspberries, and cranberries in a blender. Add the pecans (if using), agave nectar, orange zest, and ice. Blend until smooth.

FACTOID: In some places, cranberries get the nickname
"bounceberries," because ripe ones do just that: bounce!

Gazpacho Gratitude

Mary's son William and Sara's daughter Lucy came bounding home from school one day in late September to share the news that tomatoes are indeed a fruit. They both requested that we make a tomato smoothie. As it just happened to be the season when Sweet 100 tomatoes are at their peak, we quickly threw all things fresh into the blender, and the result was extraordinary! Remember, this "souper" smoothie is only as good as your tomatoes; only make it when they are fresh and ripe. For a richer taste and a probiotic hit, try adding a dollop of Greek yogurt to this savory blend.

MAKES ABOUT 2 1/2 CUPS/600 ML; SERVES 2

2 1/2 cups/430 g **fresh cherry tomatoes**
1 **medium carrot, peeled and roughly chopped**
3/4 cup/105 g **roughly chopped organic OR English/hothouse cucumber (seeded and peeled if necessary)**
3/4 cup/130 g **roughly chopped cantaloupe**
3 tbsp **chopped red onion**
1 tbsp **fresh lemon juice**
2 tsp **good-quality extra-virgin olive oil**
5 **medium fresh basil leaves**
1/2 tsp **sea salt,** plus more to taste
Freshly ground pepper

In a blender, combine the tomatoes, carrot, cucumber, cantaloupe, onion, lemon juice, olive oil, basil, 1/2 tsp salt, and pepper to taste. Pulse until smooth but still chunky. Taste and adjust the seasoning with salt and pepper.

CHAPTER 4

PROBIOTIC POWER

PROBIOTICS ARE "GOOD" BACTERIA

similar to those naturally found in our bodies. They are contained in foods such as yogurt and kefir. The probiotic foods that have the health community buzzing are more widespread than many of us may realize. Featured in grocery stores nationwide, these products are healthful food choices for adults and kids alike. Since bacteria have a reputation for causing disease, slurping back a few billion of them a day for good health may seem, well, hard to swallow. Yet the latest research shows that probiotics are indeed friendly bacteria that can help with everything from treating urinary tract and yeast infections to reducing cancer occurrences, preventing allergies and eczema in children, and treating several gastrointestinal disorders.

Boost your immune system in the morning with **STRAWBERRIES ALL THE WHEY,** pumped up with strawberry Bifidus Regularis yogurt, or our kefir-based **APPLE-FLAX FRAPPÉ.** If you are a honey lover, whirl up our **JASMINE HONEY LASSI** made with creamy Greek yogurt, or for a quintuple quench, blend up our satiating **FIBER 5,** made with fruits, nuts, and seeds. Whip up these probiotic smoothie blends and drink to strong immune system health. Remember that all the added fiber makes a contribution as well.

STRAWBERRIES all the WHEY

Mary created this smoothie for Jackson and William when they were recovering from tonsillectomies. Nursing sore throats, they were both sent to bed with ten days' worth of antibiotics and codeine-laced Tylenol. With a generous helping of organic strawberries for a dose of fiber and antioxidants, a double dose of probiotic yogurt, and a scoop of whey protein to boost the boys' immune systems, this nutritional meal replacement led to their speedy recovery. The results were astounding—no upset tummies after all those antibiotics, no constipation from all that codeine, and a "whey" quick recovery.

MAKES ABOUT 2 1/2 CUPS/600 ML; SERVES 2

3/4 cup/170 g **strawberry Bifidus Regularis yogurt, such as Activia**
1/2 cup/120 ml **probiotic vanilla drink, such as DanActive**
2 cups/225 g **frozen strawberries**
1/4 cup/20 g **whey protein powder**

Combine the yogurt and probiotic drink in a blender. Add the strawberries and protein powder. Blend until smooth.

RASPBERRY RITUAL

You might be apprehensive about kefir and cottage cheese, but we urge you not to flip this page. The cottage cheese imparts creaminess and calcium to this blend, while the kefir gives it some necessary twang, along with a boost to your intestinal health. The added banana fortifies your Raspberry Ritual with potassium and fiber, making for sweet perfection. Our entire family is hooked on this creamy blend of goodness, and we encourage you to give it a whirl.

MAKES ABOUT 2 1/2 CUPS/600 ML; SERVES 2

3/4 cup/180 ml **raspberry kefir**
1/2 cup/120 ml **fresh-pressed apple juice**
1/3 cup/75 g **low-fat cottage cheese**
3/4 cup/85 g **frozen raspberries**
1 **frozen banana, sliced**
4 to 6 **ice cubes**

Combine the kefir, apple juice, and cottage cheese in a blender. Add the raspberries, banana, and ice. Blend until smooth.

APPLE-FLAX FRAPPÉ

This frappé is essentially a fruit-blended muesli. When white nectar-ines are at their prime, this drink is hard to beat, but other nectarines and peaches are fine substitutes. Although maple syrup is more accessible, experiment with yacon syrup, as its rich caramel flavor beautifully complements the fruit. Yacon is a glucose-free sweetener, said to aid in digestion and promote beneficial bacteria. No matter how you opt to sweeten this smoothie, an Apple-Flax Frappé a day really may keep the doctor away! Throw in a few ice cubes, if you like; this mix is suited to a chilled version.

MAKES ABOUT 2 1/2 CUPS/600 ML; SERVES 2

3/4 cup/180 ml **peach kefir**
1/2 cup/120 ml **fresh-pressed apple juice**
1 cup/115 g **diced apple**
1 cup/170 g **diced white nectarine**
1/4 cup/30 g **raw almonds, preferably soaked
   and drained (SEE PAGE 122)**
2 tbsp **rolled oats**
2 tbsp **flaxseed OR chia seeds**
1/4 tsp **ground cinnamon**
Yacon syrup (SEE NOTE) OR maple syrup

Combine the kefir and apple juice in a blender. Add the apple, nectarine, almonds, oats, flaxseed, and cinnamon. Blend until smooth. Sweeten with yacon syrup.

NOTE: Yacon syrup is pressed from the root of the yacon, a distant relative of the sunflower. It has been consumed in the Andean highlands of Peru for centuries.

Jasmine Honey Lassi

Sara adds a spoonful of bee pollen granules to this flowery smoothie, which she thinks turns it over-the-top sublime. Bee pollen is a storehouse of all naturally occurring multivitamins, proteins, minerals, amino acids, enzymes, and hormones. Mary, however, is not wild about bee pollen's sweet-but-raw earthiness and chalky texture. With or without a dash of pollen, the BEE-ootiful combination of jasmine and pure raw honey calls to mind the rare deliciousness of wild honeysuckle. Remember, the floral splendor of this smoothie lies in the quality of honey that you use. If you prefer a fruitier flavor, mango-peach tea works well, too. Feel free to use frozen peaches as a substitute when fresh peaches are out of season.

MAKES ABOUT 2 1/2 CUPS/600 ML; SERVES 2

3 tbsp **raw honey**
1/2 cup/120 ml **warm strong-brewed jasmine tea**
1 1/2 cups/255 g **diced peaches**
3/4 cup/170 g **low-fat Greek yogurt**
4 to 6 **ice cubes**

Dissolve the honey in the warm tea. Refrigerate until chilled. Combine the sweetened tea, peaches, yogurt, and ice in a blender. Blend until smooth.

PURPLE HAZE

Purple Haze is as voluptuous and delicious as it is healthful. Blue-berries serve as antioxidant heavyweights, but raw almonds throw in some muscle power, too. Raw almonds have more arginine—an amino acid that boosts the immune system and inhibits tumor growth—than any other nut. They are also the only nuts that alkalize the blood, which, according to research, contributes to a strong immune system.

MAKES ABOUT 2 1/2 CUPS/600 ML; SERVES 2

1 cup/225 g **low-fat lemon yogurt**
3/4 cup/180 ml **blueberry juice, chilled**
1 cup/115 g **frozen blueberries**
1/4 cup/30 g **raw almonds, preferably soaked and drained (SEE PAGE 122)**
2 to 4 **ice cubes**

Combine the yogurt and blueberry juice in a blender. Add the blueberries, almonds, and ice. Blend until smooth.

FIBER 5

If you are thinking to yourself, "UGGGGHHH, a prune and bran smoothie . . . yucko!" we beg you to reconsider. This fiber-filled smoothie poured over a bowl of granola or bran cereal and topped with fresh blueberries is a fabulous start to any day. A high-fiber diet may help prevent diabetes, heart disease, cancer, and weight gain, not to mention the most immediate and gratifying effect of keeping you plum regular! The probiotic vanilla drink adds a fantastic twang to this morning blend, but plain kefir and yogurt also works well.

MAKES ABOUT 2 1/2 CUPS/600 ML; SERVES 2

3/4 cup/180 ml **vanilla kefir OR probiotic vanilla drink, such as DanActive**
3/4 cup/180 ml **fresh-pressed apple juice**
1/4 cup/40 g **rehydrated prunes** (SEE NOTE)
1 **frozen banana, sliced**
1/4 cup/20 g **bran-flake cereal, rolled oats, OR sprouted live organic granola**
1/4 cup/30 g **raw walnuts, preferably soaked and drained**
1 tbsp **ground flaxseed**
6 to 8 **ice cubes**

Combine the kefir, apple juice, and prunes in a blender. Add the banana, cereal, walnuts, flaxseed, and ice. Blend until smooth.

NOTE: Nutrient-rich prunes have an antioxidant score of 2,428—more than blueberries, which clock in at 1,760.

CHAPTER 5

ESSENTIAL GREENS

Enter this chapter with eyes wide open: going green in the blender can change your life. After reading *Green for Life* by Victoria Boutenko, we have become obsessed with getting more greens in our diet, so blending a green smoothie has become a daily ritual for us. Research shows that leafy greens, chock-full of chlorophyll, possess more valuable nutrients (vitamins C, K, and A; potassium; iron; fiber) than any other food group. Simply put,

THE MORE GREENS YOU EAT, THE BETTER YOU FEEL;

and you may live longer, too. Chlorophyll—to list just a few of its possible healing properties—promotes alkalinity, counteracts toxins, helps purify the liver, cleans and deodorizes bowel tissue, and even eliminates bad breath. We could go on and on.

There is no better way of consuming chlorophyll than drinking green smoothies. When greens are blended (as opposed to chewed), the nutrients are more efficiently absorbed, thus providing optimum assimilation into the body. A high-speed blender is particularly effective for the smoothies in this chapter, but if you don't have one, just expect the smoothies to be a bit chunky. Our **APPLE, CUKE, PARSLEY, MINT** is a perfectly sublime blend for morning, noon, or night. **KALE, APPLE, CARROT** will make you feel out of this world. Try our alkalinizing PINEAPPLE, ARUGULA, MACADAMIA NUT smoothie and we swear, you'll be set free. The more chlorophyll-kissed green smoothies you drink, the better you will feel and the fewer cravings you will have. We guarantee it!

APPLE, CUKE, PARSLEY, MINT

Our foodie mom came to California while we were testing recipes for this book, and she stuck her nose up at the mere thought of our experimental veggie combos. Incorporating ingredients like parsley, spinach, sugar snap peas—and hemp seed, no less!—seemed to infuriate our oh-so-spirited mother. Long story short, she has been calling us from North Carolina saying that she craves this invigoratingly fresh and vibrant blend of apples, cucumbers, and mint. Don't you just hate people who say "I told you so . . ."?

MAKES ABOUT 2 1/2 CUPS/600 ML; SERVES 2

1 cup/240 ml **fresh-pressed apple juice**

1 cup/240 ml **filtered water**

1 small **tart green apple, such as Granny Smith, cored and diced**

1/2 cup/70 g **roughly chopped organic OR English/hothouse cucumber (seeded and peeled if necessary)**

1 cup/30 g **firmly packed fresh flat-leaf (Italian) parsley leaves**

1 cup/30 g **firmly packed fresh mint leaves**

3 tbsp **hemp seeds**

Combine the apple juice, water, apple, cucumber, parsley, mint, and hemp seeds in a blender. Blend until smooth.

Kale, Apple, Carrot

This veggie blend rocks our world. Though it may seem like a grown-up blend, even our littlest tyke, Johnny Red, adores it! We love it even more knowing that the lovely leaves of the kale plant provide more nutritional value for fewer calories than almost any other food around. We keep purchased carrot juice on hand for convenience to avoid pulling out both the juicer and the blender. Use this recipe as a launching pad for other creative blends. We sometimes add chopped fresh ginger, other times fresh parsley, spinach, chard, or even Brussel sprouts (1/2 cup/55 g, quartered, for this recipe); we sometimes also substitute extra-virgin olive oil for the flaxseed oil. Kale-app-carrot is a divine combination and insanely healthful, too, but customize this recipe to suit your buds.

MAKES ABOUT 3 CUPS/720 ML; SERVES 2

---

1 1/2 cups/360 ml **fresh-pressed carrot juice**
1/2 cup/120 ml **filtered water**
1 cup/30 g **firmly packed chopped kale leaves,
   tough stems and spines removed**
1 small **apple, cored and diced**
2 tbsp **raw sunflower seeds**
1 tbsp **fresh lemon juice**
1 tbsp **flaxseed oil**

Combine the carrot juice, water, kale, apple, sunflower seeds, lemon juice, and flaxseed oil in a blender. Blend until smooth.

PERSIMMON, CRANBERRY, SPINACH

Ultra-sweet persimmons, super-tart cranberries, and spicy ginger make a sexy ménage à trois. And the raw spinach adds an unobtrusive backdrop of green energy that your body craves. There are two common types of persimmon: Fuyu, the crisp kind you can eat right away, and Hachiya, the kind you can't. A Hachiya persimmon is ready to eat only when very soft, like a squishy water balloon with no firm spots; less-than-ripe specimens will make your smoothie astringent and bitter. Persimmons are not only high in fiber and vitamins A and C, but are also thought to have anticancer properties, as do the spinach and cranberries here. When you know that you could be protecting yourself from the C word while consuming all this bounty, you may feel the urge to do a little happy dance right there in your kitchen!

MAKES ABOUT 3 CUPS/720 ML; SERVES 2

1 cup/240 ml **fresh-pressed apple juice**
$^1/_2$ cup/120 ml **filtered water**
Pulp of 1 medium **very soft Hachiya persimmon**
    (about $^3/_4$ cup/130 g)
$^1/_2$ cup/55 g **fresh cranberries**
1 $^1/_2$ cups/40 g **firmly packed spinach leaves,**
    tough stems removed
1 tsp **peeled and chopped fresh ginger**

Combine the apple juice, water, persimmon pulp, cranberries, spinach, and ginger in a blender. Blend until smooth.

NOTE: Firm Hachiya persimmons can be ripened further by keeping them at room temperature for a week or more. To accelerate ripening, put them in a bag with a banana. The ethylene gas produced by the banana will help ripen the persimmons.

PINEAPPLE, ARUGULA, Macadamia NUT

Trust us, this combination is super-clean and green, refreshing and yummy. The alkalinizing fresh pineapple pairs beautifully with the spice of the arugula/rocket. And macadamia nuts are a high-energy food that adds a crunchy rich texture and a healthy dose of protein and fiber (we don't mind at all if they do not fully incorporate) as well as monounsaturated fatty acids—or "good" fat—that significantly reduce blood serum cholesterol levels. Think of this smoothie as a cleansing, satisfying meal replacement. Get to know chia seeds. These miraculous little seeds are a form of easily digestible protein that is full of minerals, vitamins, and soluble fiber. Rich in omega fatty acids, and similar to flaxseed, chia seeds have the significant advantage of being more stable.

MAKES ABOUT 3 CUPS/720 ML; SERVES 2

3/4 cup/180 ml **filtered water**
1 cup/240 ml **fresh-pressed apple juice**
1 1/2 cups/255 g **chopped fresh pineapple, chilled**
3/4 cup/20 g **firmly packed arugula/rocket,
   tough stems removed**
3/4 cup/20 g **firmly packed fresh mint leaves**
2 tbsp **roughly chopped raw macadamia nuts**
2 tbsp **chia seeds OR flax seeds**
Pinch of **sea salt**

Combine the water, apple juice, pineapple, arugula/rocket, mint, macadamia nuts, chia seeds, and salt in a blender. Blend until smooth.

FACTOID: Chia seeds create a physical barrier between carbohydrates and the digestive enzymes that break them down, thus slowing the conversion of carbohydrates into sugar.

ORANGE, SUGAR SNAP PEA, PUMPKIN SEED

After a celebratory weekend, a Monday-morning cleanse is often what the doctor ordered. After a work-your-booty-off winter boot camp, we blended vitamin C–packed navel oranges with fresh mint and, for a fresh twist, sugar snap peas. A handful of raw pumpkin seeds and a drizzle of extra-virgin olive oil add a dose of healthful fat as well as a burst of antioxidants. And a dash of cayenne, considered a warming ingredient, may boost the metabolism. Though the ingredient list is unusual, this light, hydrating, and nutrient-dense smoothie is perfect to get you back on track after a splurge of a weekend!

MAKES ABOUT 3 CUPS/720 ML; SERVES 2

1 cup/170 g **orange segments with their juice, chilled**

1 cup/60 g **raw sugar snap peas, stems and strings removed**

1 cup/240 ml **fresh-pressed apple juice**

3/4 cup/180 ml **filtered water**

1/2 cup/15 g **firmly packed fresh mint leaves**

3 tbsp **raw pumpkin seeds**

2 tbsp **chia seeds**

1 tsp **extra-virgin olive oil**

Pinch of **cayenne pepper**

Combine the oranges and their juice, the peas, apple juice, water, mint, pumpkin seeds, chia seeds, olive oil, and cayenne in a blender. Blend until smooth.

CARROT, BEET, WATERCRESS

We have always loved a watercress salad with beetroots, apples, and almonds, so why not throw these complementary ingredients into a blender with wholesome sweet carrot juice and a squeeze of lemon? We did, and this exquisite salad smoothie was born. Watercress has a unique chemical, phenethyt isothiocyanate, with the acronym PEITC, which has been found to prevent cancer growth at various stages critical to tumor development. Knowing this makes watercress all the more beloved in our culinary repertoire, but if you are not a watercress lover, lettuce, spinach, or fresh mint make fine alternatives.

MAKES ABOUT 3 CUPS/720 ML; SERVES 2

1 1/2 cups/360 ml **fresh-pressed carrot juice**
1/2 cup/120 ml **filtered water**
1 cup/30 g **firmly packed watercress, tough stems removed**
1/2 cup/70 g **grated raw beets/beetroots**
1/2 **red apple, cored and roughly chopped**
2 tbsp **raw almonds, preferably soaked and drained** (SEE PAGE 122)
2 tbsp **fresh lemon juice**
1 tsp **flaxseed oil**

Combine the carrot juice, water, watercress, beets/beetroots, apple, almonds, lemon juice, and flaxseed oil in a blender. Blend until smooth.

NOTE: A study published in *Cancer Research* in 2007 showed that the presence of PEITC in watercress inhibited the growth of human colon and prostate cancer cells. Studies have also shown evidence that PEITC can block the growth of breast cancer cells.

TOMATO, RED PEPPER, PARSLEY, LIME

Let's face it, basil, mint, and cilantro/fresh coriander are always stealing the limelight from poor parsley. Often ignored in its popular role as a table garnish, parsley finally gets the homage it deserves in this veggie blend. Not only does parsley have a vibrant, celery-like taste that so jives with tomatoes, lime, and jalapeño, it also has healing properties. Parsley's volatile oils qualify it as a "chemo-protective" food, a food that can help neutralize particular carcinogens. In animal studies, parsley has been shown to inhibit tumor formation. We prefer the more pungent Italian, or flat-leaf, parsley to the curly kind, as it has more flavor. Enjoy this vegetable blend and you may agree with us that parsley is indeed a culinary rock star!

MAKES ABOUT 2 1/2 CUPS/600 ML; SERVES 2

3/4 cup **Sweet 100s** OR **other cherry tomatoes**

1 cup/240 ml **fresh-pressed carrot juice**

1/4 cup/60 ml **filtered water**

1 cup/30 g **firmly packed fresh flat-leaf (Italian) parsley leaves**

1 small **red bell pepper/capsicum, seeded and roughly chopped**

2 tbsp **raw pine nuts**

1 tbsp **fresh lime juice,** plus more to taste

1 tbsp **extra-virgin olive oil**

1 tsp **chopped seeded jalapeño,** plus more to taste

1/4 tsp **sea salt,** plus more to taste

Combine the tomatoes, carrot juice, and water in a blender. Add the parsley, bell pepper/capsicum, pine nuts, 1 tbsp lime juice, the olive oil, 1 tsp jalapeño, and 1/4 tsp salt. Blend until smooth. Taste and adjust the seasoning with lime juice, salt, and jalapeño.

CHAPTER 6

Family Faves

Though it is nearly impossible to single out our favorites,

THIS IS OUR SHORT LIST OF TRIED-AND-TRUE TREASURES.

We have all come to an agreement that these recipes are among the best we Corpening sisters have in our repertoire! They please kids and parents alike, not only for their yum factor but also for their contribution to good health and wellness.

Our little rug rats swoon over **COCONUT DREAM CREAM,** our healthful raw rendition of crème anglaise without the eggs, sugar, and cream. It is so creamy and rich it will blow your mind! William, Mary's middle son, boasts about **PASSION BERRY BLISS,** a staple in the Barber household that he and Mary randomly concocted one day after school. It since has become a favorite of Sara's girls, too, and each kid customizes the blend with varying amounts of agave nectar. Our husbands are coffee addicts, so their fondness for **RASPBERRY CAPPUCCINO** is unmistakable. We, on the other hand, are tea totalers and pay homage with **NAKED ANGEL ICED TEA,** a minty fresh blend that we created for Dlush, a youth beverage joint in San Diego. From our house to yours, let our faves become some of yours.

Acai Colada

The subtle addition of acai jacks up this smoothie's ORAC (oxygen radical absorption capacity) value, which is a fancy way of measuring antioxidants that help fight the ravages of free radicals. For years we made smoothies like this one with fresh pineapple that we peeled, chopped, and froze ourselves. Now, pineapple is conveniently pre-packaged in the frozen section of most grocery stores. Look out for an array of acai juice blends as well. Although this smoothie stands tall on its own, adding a splash of rum is YUMMMMM . . .

MAKES ABOUT 2 1/2 CUPS/600 ML; SERVES 2

1 cup/240 ml **acai-blueberry juice, such as Bossa Nova**
1 **fresh ripe banana**
1 1/2 cups/255 g **chopped frozen pineapple**
3/4 cup/170 g **coconut sorbet**
2 to 3 drops **coconut extract/essence**

Combine the acai-blueberry juice and banana in a blender. Add the pineapple, sorbet, and coconut extract/essence. Blend until smooth.

SWEET 'n' SALTY PEANUT CRUNCH

Forgive yourself in advance for this indulgence and savor each crunchy sip knowing that peanut butter packs a serious nutritional punch and offers a variety of health benefits. Numerous studies have shown that this small legume is a big ally to healthy hearts. Peanuts are also a very good source of monounsaturated fats and of vitamin E, niacin, folate, protein, and manganese.

MAKES ABOUT 2 1/2 CUPS/600 ML; SERVES 2

3/4 cup/180 ml **hazelnut milk** (PAGE 127) **OR almond milk** (PAGE 122)
1/3 cup/95 g **natural peanut butter**
1/2 cup/115 g **low-fat vanilla frozen yogurt**
1 **frozen banana**
2 tsp **vanilla extract/essence**
1/2 tsp **sea salt**
4 to 6 **ice cubes**
1/3 cup/45 g **raw almonds**

Combine the hazelnut milk, peanut butter, frozen yogurt, banana, vanilla, salt, and ice in a blender. Blend until smooth. Add the almonds and pulse a few times, just until incorporated but still crunchy.

PASSION BERRY BLISS

This smoothie is William Barber's favorite smoothie in the world.
He created the recipe years ago, and it is a Barber family staple.
William chose vanilla yogurt in this recipe, as he is an avid vanilla fan,
but this smoothie also works well with strawberry or raspberry yogurt.
Add agave nectar to suit your taste buds, as brands of juice and
yogurt and bags of frozen fruit all vary in their level of tartness.

MAKES ABOUT 2 1/2 CUPS/600 ML; SERVES 2

1/2 cup/120 ml **passion-fruit juice**
1/2 cup/ 115 g **low-fat vanilla yogurt**
1 **fresh ripe banana**
1 cup/115 g **frozen strawberries**
1/2 cup/55 g **frozen raspberries**
1 tbsp **agave nectar,** plus more to taste

Combine the passion-fruit juice and yogurt in a blender.
Add the banana, strawberries, raspberries, and 1 tbsp agave
nectar. Blend until smooth. Taste and add more agave nectar,
if you like.

COCONUT DREAM CREAM

If you think this ingredient list sounds too twiggy and barky, try it anyway. We were intimidated by Thai young coconuts until the day when Sara locked carts at Whole Foods with a lady who was purchasing ten of them, and her curiosity was piqued. The lady jubilantly explained that Thai young coconuts had cured her of a twenty-year mold affliction. One a day kept her life-altering allergy away. Even though we don't have allergies, these gems are now a staple in our households as well. Once you learn how easy it is to extract the water and the flesh, you will wish you had discovered this sacred superfood sooner. Morton Satin, formerly chief for the Food and Agriculture Organization of the United Nations, said, "Coconut water is the very stuff of nature, biologically pure, full of natural sugars, salts, and vitamins to ward off fatigue . . . and is the next wave of energy drinks—but natural!"

MAKES ABOUT 2 1/2 CUPS/600 ML; SERVES 2

1 1/2 cups/360 ml **coconut milk, blended from water and meat of 1 Thai young coconut** (SEE NOTE, PAGE 46)

2 to 4 **Medjool dates, pits removed**

1/2 tsp **vanilla extract/essence**

Pinch of **sea salt**

1/2 cup/120 ml **hazelnut milk (PAGE 127) OR almond milk (PAGE 122), chilled,** plus more as needed

Combine the coconut milk, dates, vanilla, and salt. Blend until smooth. Blend in the hazelnut milk. Add more hazelnut milk to thin to the desired consistency, if necessary.

Naked Angel Iced Tea

Since its inception, we have developed recipes for Dlush, a sleek youth beverage joint headquartered in San Diego. This recipe is a smoothie version of Dlush's signature Naked Angel Iced Tea. Our rendition has fresh mango, which is rich in vitamin A and has healthful amounts of vitamins B and C, potassium, and iron. This wildly satisfying smoothie is a thrill to the palate as well as a boost to health and well-being.

MAKES ABOUT 2 1/2 CUPS/600 ML; SERVES 2

1 1/2 cups/255 g **diced mango**
3/4 cup/180 ml **passion-fruit juice**
1 cup/240 ml **strong-brewed Earl Grey tea, made into ice cubes**
8 **medium fresh mint leaves**
1/4 tsp **vanilla extract/essence**
Agave nectar
Fresh lemon juice

Combine the mango and passion-fruit juice in a blender. Add the Earl Grey ice cubes, mint, and vanilla. Blend until smooth. Blend in agave nectar and lemon juice to taste.

RASPBERRY CAPPUCCINO

Mary first discovered the beauty of cold-brew coffee when her third son, John, was born. John McCulloch, John's dear godfather, delivered a gallon of it as a "mama" gift shortly after the baby's arrival. Sleep-deprived and off-the-charts busy, Mary quickly developed an afternoon addiction to this life-saving overnight-drip coffee. When she ran out, she tried to resume her traditional coffee habit but just couldn't. After discovering the sublime smoothness of cold-brew coffee, and learning that it is nearly 70 percent less acidic than traditional coffee, Mary and Sara will never turn back. We urge you to order some online and see for yourself.

MAKES ABOUT 2 1/2 CUPS/600 ML; SERVES 2

3/4 cup/180 ml **cold low-fat chocolate milk**
1/3 cup/75 ml **cold-brew coffee** (SEE PAGE 126),
   strong-brewed coffee, or espresso, cooled to
   room temperature or chilled
3/4 cup/170 g **chocolate sorbet**
1 1/2 cups/170 g **frozen unsweetened strawberries**
3/4 cup/85 g **frozen unsweetened raspberries**
1/2 cup/120 ml **cold low-fat plain milk**
Unsweetened cocoa powder for garnish

Combine the chocolate milk, coffee, sorbet, strawberries, and raspberries in a blender. Blend until smooth. Pour into two glasses. Rinse out the blender jar. Pour the plain milk into the blender and blend on high speed until frothy, about 15 seconds. Divide between the smoothies and sprinkle with cocoa powder.

CHAPTER 7

LIGHT and LUSCIOUS

THE BLENDS IN THIS CHAPTER ARE SKIMPY ON CALORIES BUT NOT ON FLAVOR.

These delightfully light and satisfying smoothies are for the calorie conscious, for those who crave a light pre- or post-workout snack, and for those in need of a hydrating injection.

Try the **ELECTROLYTE ELIXIR** for a restorative thirst quencher that's so invigorating it may even inspire you to get off the couch. For a highly satisfying, light, and luscious lunch, try our **GREEK GODDESS.** The **MUCHO MATCHA** promises to cleanse your system while satisfying your taste buds. Our melon smoothies, **WATERMELON AGUA FRESCA** and **MELON MOJO,** are both guilt free and delicious, so know that you can drink to your heart's content and still render your body slender!

watermelon agua fresca

Traditionally, authentic agua frescas are made without blenders, by simply mashing fruit with a fork or masher before adding water. We've taken the liberty of using a blender for an ultra-light, refreshing rendition of this traditional Mexican drink. In the spring and summer, we use fresh strawberries and a few ice cubes in lieu of the frozen ones for ultimate freshness.

MAKES ABOUT 2 1/2 CUPS/600 ML; SERVES 2

3 cups/450 g **diced seeded watermelon, chilled**
1 cup/115 g **frozen strawberries**
1 tbsp **fresh lemon juice**
Pinch of **sea salt**
Agave nectar (optional)

Combine the watermelon, strawberries, lemon juice, and salt in a blender. Blend until smooth. Sweeten with agave nectar, if you like.

Pineapple Pizzazz

Pineapple adds pizzazz to the classic peach-melba combination featuring raspberries and peaches. Pineapple and raspberries are both rich sources of vitamin C and manganese, which help prevent damage to cell membranes and other structures in the body by neutralizing free radicals. Drink this delectable blend and all those antioxidants may help reverse the ravages of age.

MAKES ABOUT 2 1/2 CUPS/600 ML; SERVES 2

1 cup/240 ml **peach nectar**
3/4 cup/85 g **fresh raspberries**
1/4 **fresh ripe banana**
1 3/4 cups/300 g **chopped frozen pineapple**

Combine the peach nectar and raspberries in a blender. Add the banana and pineapple. Blend until smooth.

ELECTROLYTE ELIXIR

This combination of fresh watermelon and electrolyte-enhanced water is a thirst-quenching electrolyte rush. Both watermelon and vitamin water are chock-full of electrolytes (calcium, potassium, and magnesium), which are lost through perspiration during exercise. Watermelon is also rich in B vitamins necessary for energy production, which makes this smoothie a perfect pre- and post-workout blend.

MAKES ABOUT 2 1/2 CUPS/600 ML; SERVES 2

1 1/2 cups/215 g **diced seeded watermelon, chilled**
1/2 cup/55 g **fresh raspberries**
1 cup/240 ml **berry-flavored enhanced water, such as Vitamin Water (SEE NOTE), made into ice cubes**
1 tbsp **agave nectar,** plus more as needed
2 tsp **fresh lemon juice**
Pinch of **sea salt**

Combine the watermelon, raspberries, and enhanced-water ice cubes in a blender. Add the 1 tbsp agave nectar, the lemon juice, and the salt. Blend until smooth. Taste and add more agave nectar, if you like.

NOTE: In response to negative press about refined sugars, corn-syrup sweeteners, and artificial flavorings, there are many new, health-inspired waters "enhanced" with electrolytes, vitamins, and other extras on the market. Feel free to use your favorite flavor, but we think that the red drinks taste best with this smoothie.

MUCHO MATCHA

This matcha mango smoothie has a tropical flavor with green tea essence and a hit of ginger. It is as delicious as it is cleansing. The high chlorophyll and mineral content of the matcha make it a strong blood detoxifier and alkalinizer, as well as an effective blood sugar stabilizer. The addition of ginger makes this shake even more detoxifying, because ginger has been used for years as a cleansing agent to the bowels, kidneys, and skin. So get your green on and make this detoxifying elixir a part of your life.

MAKES ABOUT 2 1/2 CUPS/600 ML; SERVES 2

1 cup/225 g **low-fat mango-apricot yogurt**
1/2 cup/120 ml **vanilla soy milk**
1 1/4 cups/215 g **chopped frozen mango**
3/4 cup/180 ml **passion-fruit juice, made into ice cubes**
1 tsp **matcha powder, plus more to taste**
3/4 tsp **peeled and chopped fresh ginger**

Combine the yogurt and soy milk in a blender. Add the mango, passion-fruit ice cubes, 1 tsp matcha powder, and the ginger. Blend until smooth. Add more matcha powder, if you like.

FACTOID: Green tea is well known for its health properties, but matcha contains up to 137 times more antioxidants. Pound for pound, it has the highest level of antioxidants (measured in ORAC units) of any food on Earth.

MELON MOJO

It's no wonder honeydew is called the temptation melon, as it delivers unparalleled sweetness at only 60 calories per cup. Its sweetness is balanced here by the subtle tartness of kiwis and grapes. Lime juice introduces another tart note, while the pinch of salt heightens the overall flavor. The result: a perfect sweet-tart punch. A healthy dose of vitamin C and folate makes this melon mojo fantastic for women of child-bearing age. If you do not want the kiwi seeds to break down, blend this smoothie in a food processor.

MAKES ABOUT 2 1/2 CUPS/600 ML; SERVES 2

2 cups/340 g **diced honeydew melon, chilled**
1 cup/170 g **frozen white grapes**
1 tsp **fresh lime juice,** plus more to taste
Pinch of **sea salt**
4 to 6 **ice cubes**
1 cup/170 g **diced kiwi** (about 3)

Combine the honeydew, grapes, 1 tsp lime juice, the salt, and ice in a blender or food processor. Blend until smooth. Add the kiwi and pulse until just incorporated. Taste and add more lime juice, if you like.

BLUEBERRY-ACAI MOUSSE

After eating a sumptuous chocolate-hazelnut mousse at our favorite raw-food restaurant, Café Gratitude, we learned that it was Irish moss that lent the dessert its amazing texture. Already curious about this iodine-rich red algae from the Atlantic, we took a class on it and learned that working with Irish moss is remarkably easy. Our recipe requires a high-speed blender, because the Irish moss must be fully pulverized for this miraculous and voluptuous smoothie to be at its best. In addition to acting as a flavorless natural thickener, Irish moss touts myriad health claims, from increased thyroid function to weight loss. Even better, it expands in your stomach, creating a satiating "full effect" that's a boon for dieters.

MAKES ABOUT 2 1/2 CUPS/600 ML; SERVES 2

1/2 cup/30 g **rinsed, soaked, and drained Irish moss**
    (SEE PAGE 128)
3/4 cup/180 ml **almond milk** (PAGE 122)
3/4 cup/180 ml **pomegranate juice**
3/4 cup/85 g **blueberries**
One 3 1/2-oz/100-g **frozen acai smoothie pack,** OR
    1 cup/225 g **acai sorbet**
1/2 **frozen banana, sliced**

Gently shake the Irish moss to remove any excess water. Combine the Irish moss and almond milk in a blender. Starting on low speed and gradually raising it to the highest speed, blend until the moss is completely emulsified and there are absolutely no detectable specks, 1 to 2 minutes. The mixture will get slightly warm. Immediately add the pomegranate juice, blueberries, sorbet, and banana and blend until smooth. Drink immediately, or refrigerate for up to 24 hours for a thicker version.

NOTE: We are fans of Irish moss, but this recipe is delicious without it. It will have a juicy consistency rather than a fluffy, mousselike one.

SKINNY ME

This slenderizer is good to your waistline and tough on colds, but its flavor springs from the zing of citrus. With fewer than 150 calories, this blend can help you manage your weight, protect your immune system, cool your pipes, and even leave you with minty fresh breath.

MAKES ABOUT 2 1/2 CUPS/600 ML; SERVES 2

1 1/2 cups/255 g **orange segments with their juice**
1/2 cup/85 g **grapefruit segments with their juice**
1 cup/240 ml **brewed peppermint tea, made into ice cubes**
1/4 cup/10 g **firmly packed fresh mint leaves**
2 tbsp **agave nectar**

Combine the orange and grapefruit segments with their juices and the peppermint-tea ice cubes in a blender. Add the mint and agave nectar. Blend until smooth.

FACTOID: One medium orange supplies about 150 percent of the daily value of vitamin C.

GReeK GODDeSS

After a five-hour run of testing smoothies, Mary exclaimed, "We've struck brilliance!" This has become our favorite lunch smoothie. It is designed for those with hypoglycemia and diabetes, as it is extremely low in sugar and high in protein. Cottage cheese hides nicely in smoothies because it blends instantly into a creamy delight. Enjoy this tart and tangy cucumber blend with hints of mint, hues of green/spring onion, and crisp green apple. You may feel inclined to put this one in a bowl.

MAKES ABOUT 2 1/2 CUPS/600 ML; SERVES 2

1/2 cup/120 ml **filtered water**
1/2 cup/115 g **low-fat Greek yogurt**
1 cup/140 g **roughly chopped seeded organic**
   OR English/hothouse cucumber (seeded and
   peeled if necessary)
1/2 cup/85 g **frozen green grapes**
1/4 cup/20 g **chopped green/spring onions,**
   tender green parts only
10 **medium fresh mint leaves,** plus more to taste
1 tbsp **fresh lemon juice,** plus more to taste
1/4 tsp **sea salt,** plus more to taste
1 cup/115 g **chopped green apple**
1/2 cup **cottage cheese**

Combine the water, yogurt, cucumber, grapes, green/spring onions, 10 mint leaves, 1 tbsp lemon juice, and 1/4 tsp salt in a blender. Blend until smooth. Add the apple and cottage cheese and pulse a few times, just until incorporated. Taste and adjust the seasoning with mint, lemon juice, and salt.

CHAPTER 8

KID-LICIOUS

SMOOTHIES ARE PERFECT FOOD FOR KIDS OF ALL AGES,

not only because they're yummy, but because they are so much fun to make together. Our kids have chosen their favorite concoctions for this chapter. Whether you serve these smoothies for breakfast, as snacks, or as a healthful dessert, these are drink combinations that parents can feel good about.

SMARTY PANTS has a shot of DHA omega fatty acid, sure to feed a kid's growing brain, and **PINK-A-LICIOUS** has a handful of cashews for a hidden boost of protein. When making **PEANUT BANANA FOFANA,** we alternate between using soft silken tofu and cottage cheese. Our **SASSY STRAWBERRY GRANOLA CRUNCH** was a real breakthrough: Why did it take us so long to realize that blending granola into a smoothie or sprinkling it on top is so delicious? This has become a ritual in our households using a variety of smoothies and organic sprouted live granolas.

This chapter is near and dear to our hearts, as each of our children has sat on the counter, blended away, and discussed what they liked or didn't like in each recipe. Each smoothie had to pass their test, so thumbs up to our little tasters. We hope smoothie-making elicits the same enthusiasm for testing and tasting from your kids.

Orange Julia

As children, we had a fetish for the popular sweet-and-creamy *Orange Julius*. We now make this healthier rendition for our kids during the winter months when citrus is in season and runny noses are rampant. While the whey protein and nonfat dry milk make this drink delectably creamy, they also add a healthy dose of protein and calcium, which help support overall growth and bone health. With a host of antioxidants such as vitamin C, the Orange Julia is a germ-busting improvement on the beloved old Julius.

MAKES ABOUT 2 1/2 CUPS/600 ML; SERVES 2

---

1 1/4 cups/255 g **orange segments with their juice**
3/4 cup/170 g **tangerine sorbet** (SEE NOTE)
2 tsp **fresh lemon juice,** plus more to taste
4 to 6 **ice cubes**
1/4 cup/20 g **whey protein powder**
3 tbsp **nonfat dry milk powder**

Combine the oranges and their juice, the sorbet, 2 tsp lemon juice, and the ice in a blender. Blend until smooth. Pulse in the whey protein and milk powders. Taste and add more lemon juice, if you like.

NOTE: If you can't find tangerine sorbet, orange sherbet makes a fine substitute.

SMARTY PANTS

The gals in the Whiteford household love to say, "Boys go to Jupiter to get more stupider, and girls go to college to get more knowledge!" And, of course, at the Barbers' household of boys, the reverse is their mantra. Anyway you say it, the omega-3 fatty acids in this smoothie are critical for a healthy brain. They come in the form of children's DHA (docosahexaenoic acid), which can be found in most natural foods stores. Hard to get down by itself, the supplement's cod-liver-oil flavor is beautifully concealed in this smoothie, so your lil' smarty pants won't know it is there, supporting his or her memory, learning ability, focus, and visual development.

MAKES ABOUT 2 1/2 CUPS/600 ML; SERVES 2

3/4 cup/170 g **low-fat blueberry yogurt**
1/2 cup/120 ml **Concord grape juice**
1 1/2 cups/255 g **frozen red grapes**
1/2 cup/55 g **frozen raspberries**
1 tsp **omega-3 supplement, such as Nordic Naturals Children's DHA**

Combine the yogurt, grape juice, grapes, and raspberries in a blender. Blend until smooth. Add the omega-3 supplement and pulse until well blended.

peanut Banana FOFana

The first time we made this smoothie for the kids, we sneaked in the tofu. No need to sneak now, as this delectable blend has received kudos from nearly every kid in both of our neighborhoods. We told them about the tofu after the fact, and they all grew wide-eyed in disbelief. The boys especially loved knowing that tofu can make them buff, as it is loaded with protein and free of cholestorol. The girls, on the other hand, seemed a tad more interested in the omega-3 fatty acid effect. They would rather down this yummy, nutty blend of brain food than a piece of salmon any day. We didn't bother telling them that peanut butter is an excellent source of methionine, an essential amino acid that plays a role in cognitive function and neurological activity.

MAKES ABOUT 2 1/2 CUPS/600 ML; SERVES 2

3/4 cup/180 ml **vanilla soy milk**
1/2 cup/115 g **soft silken tofu OR low-fat cottage cheese**
1/3 cup/95 g **natural peanut butter**
2 **frozen bananas, sliced**
2 tsp **vanilla extract/essence**
4 **ice cubes**

Combine the soy milk, silken tofu, and peanut butter in a blender. Add the bananas, vanilla, and ice. Blend until smooth.

SASSY STRAWBERRY GRANOLA CRUNCH

We love this rise-and-shine smoothie, as it has lots of presentation options. Pulse the granola into this smoothie or stir it in for a crispier effect. Our kids love this concoction served in a bowl with the granola sprinkled on top. Use a parfait glass for a sassy presentation and layer granola into this voluptuous strawberry blend. Garnish with some fresh strawberries.

MAKES ABOUT 2 1/2 CUPS/600 ML; SERVES 2

3/4 cup/170 g **low-fat vanilla yogurt**
1/2 cup/120 ml **fresh-pressed apple juice**
1 1/4 cups/140 g **frozen strawberries**
1 **frozen banana, sliced**
1/2 cup/60 g **sprouted live organic granola,**
    plus more to taste

Combine the yogurt and apple juice in a blender. Add the strawberries and banana. Blend until smooth. Pulse or stir in 1/2 cup granola until incorporated. Add more granola, if you like.

PInK-a-LICIOUS

It's no secret that nuts are a great source of protein, but did you know that eating nuts four times a week can decrease the risk of heart disease? So, we've started sneaking nuts of all kinds into smoothies. After you taste this creamy pudding-like blend, you won't believe that cashews have a lower fat content than most other nuts.

MAKES ABOUT 2 1/2 CUPS/600 ML; SERVES 2

1 cup/240 ml **fresh-pressed apple juice**
1/2 cup/55 g **raw unsalted cashews, preferably soaked and drained** (SEE PAGE 124)
1 **fresh ripe banana**
1/2 cup/55 g **fresh raspberries**
1 cup/115 g **frozen strawberries**

Combine the apple juice, cashews, and banana in a blender. Add the raspberries and strawberries. Blend until smooth.

GOODNESS GRAPENESS

This trio of grapes, blueberries, and pomegranate melds into a distinguished blend with outstanding health benefits. In fact, our kids refer to this smoothie as a "true blue antioxidant superhero." No doubt, fellow moms will feel great about whipping up Goodness Grapeness for an afternoon snack. If you can't find pomegranate sorbet, strawberry, raspberry, or acai sorbets make fine substitutes.

MAKES ABOUT 2 1/2 CUPS/600 ML; SERVES 2

1 cup/240 ml **blueberry juice**
1 cup/170 g **frozen red grapes**
3/4 cup/170 g **pomegranate sorbet**
1/2 cup/55 g **frozen blueberries**
2 to 4 **ice cubes**

Combine the blueberry juice and grapes in a blender.
Add the sorbet, blueberries, and ice. Blend until smooth.

Nectarine-y

We discovered this magical blend as little girls at Figure 8 Island, a beach in North Carolina. While the adults sipped peach daiquiris, a quest for our own cocktail spawned this virgin version. Back then we preferred peeled nectarines, but now we like to keep the peel in this smoothie, as it adds a dose of fiber and a lovely visual effect. Try this recipe with white peaches or white nectarines for a sublime alternative. Spike it with some rum if your kids have scampered off in the yard and you're in the mood for a little summer fun.

MAKES ABOUT 2 1/2 CUPS/600 ML; SERVES 2

3 1/2 cups/600 g **chopped nectarines**
1 tbsp **agave nectar** OR **sugar,** plus more to taste
2 tsp **fresh lemon juice,** plus more to taste
6 to 8 **ice cubes**

Combine the nectarines, 1 tbsp agave nectar, 2 tsp lemon juice, and ice. Blend until smooth. Taste and add more agave nectar and/or lemon juice, if you like.

Banana BuBBLe

Customize your Banana Bubble to suit your buds. We prefer bananas that are just barely ripe, with not a freckle in sight. The kids, however, choose a semifreckled banana because they love a sweeter, more intense banana flavor. Adjust the amount of ice to suit your mood; sometimes we crave the consistency of frothy iced milk and other times we load up on ice to achieve milkshake status. For variety, we sometimes add a scoop of peanut butter or almond butter, or a handful of nuts; other times we add flaxseed, wheat germ, or oatmeal.

MAKES ABOUT 2 1/2 CUPS/600 ML; SERVES 2

1 1/4 cups/300 ml **low-fat milk**
1 **fresh ripe banana**
2 tsp **vanilla extract/essence**
10 **ice cubes**
Agave nectar (optional)

Combine the milk, banana, vanilla, and ice in a blender. Blend until smooth and frothy. Sweeten with agave nectar, if you like.

NOTE: With kids spending long hours indoors and being slathered with sunscreen the moment they step out, some children may be deficient in vitamin D. Choose vitamin D–fortified milk to deliver some of what they're missing from the sun.

WaTerMeLon JIGGLY

We made this hydrating smoothie for the kids in Mary and Jack's 'hood, and their enthusiasm for this yummy refreshment was electric. The novelty of watermelon mixed with homemade gelatin delighted children of every age. We serve this thirst-quenching slurpy to the kids with a straw; for adults, we sometimes omit the gelatin for a more grown-up appeal. Whether your family prefers the wiggly-jiggly stuff or not, this one is all about yum!

MAKES ABOUT 2 ¹/2 CUPS/600 ML; SERVES 2

1 ¹/2 cups/220 g **diced seeded watermelon, chilled**
³/4 cup/85 g **frozen strawberries**
³/4 cup/180 ml **pomegranate-apple juice,**
  made into ice cubes
2 tbsp **agave nectar**
Pinch of **sea salt**
¹/2 cup/135 g **pomegranate-apple OR cherry gelatin**
  (SEE NOTE)

Combine the watermelon, strawberries, and pomegranate-apple ice cubes in a blender. Add the agave nectar and salt. Blend until smooth. Add the gelatin and pulse a few times just to break it up; the gelatin should not be fully blended, allowing its jiggle and shine to feature in the mix.

NOTE: To make your own gelatin, pour ³/4 cup/180 ml of your favorite red juice into a heatproof bowl. Sprinkle 1 package (¹/4 oz/7 g) unflavored gelatin powder over the juice and let stand for 1 minute. Add 1 cup/240 ml boiling juice and 1 tbsp agave nectar and stir until dissolved. Refrigerate until set. (If time challenged, pour the gelatin mixture into a shallow glass bowl and freeze until set, about 20 minutes.)

FACTOID: Though the main nutrient in watermelon is vitamin C, the fruit is loaded with B vitamins, which are responsible for much of the body's energy production.

CHAPTER 9

FOR GROWN-UPS ONLY

IT'S SIMPLE:

Alcohol is acidic and fruit is alkalinizing. Because it is believed that disease grows in acidic (not alkaline) environments, we make a conscientious attempt to promote alkalinity in our bodies by consuming as many veggies and fruits as we can. In this chapter, we feature oh-so-modern tipples that will make your taste buds sing and your body wanna dance!

Introduce your guests to a novel **PINEAPPLE MOJITO SLUSH,** a ground-breaking twist on the beloved classic. The **CUCUMBER SAKE-TINI,** a blend of gin, sake, lime, mint, and cucumber—yes, cucumber—is sure to surprise and delight. Perhaps one of our favorite smoothie cocktails ever is the **HONEYDEW GIMLET,** and we are not even gin lovers. Honeydew, green grapes, gin, lime, and basil will dazzle your guests and inspire great conversation. ACAI SANGRIA is sure to rock your world and your guests', too. Let's face it, a memorable party centers around a memorable cocktail, so rev up your blender and show off your new repertoire of smoothie cocktails. We make big batches several hours in advance and store them in the freezer. We always want our guests to be well served, yet we don't want to be bogged down in the kitchen during the festivities.

CUCUMBER sake-TINI

Kathy Casey is one of Seattle's most talented chefs, and this cucumber sake-tini was inspired by her specialty drink, the Katana. We warn you that this martini is absolutely lethal, because the cooling cucumber masks the potency of the gin. The sake adds a little je ne sais quoi and the mint heightens the overall floral bouquet. The result is a drink that is sooooooooooo sippable that it's hard to stop. Due to popular demand, we often serve this at our Southern supper club.

MAKES ABOUT 2 1/2 CUPS/600 ML; SERVES 2

3/4 cup/180 ml **gin**
1/4 cup/60 ml **premium sake**
1/4 cup/60 ml **fresh lime juice**
2 cups/280 g **peeled, seeded, and diced cucumber, frozen**
1/2 cup/85 g **green grapes, frozen**
1/4 cup/10 g **firmly packed fresh mint leaves**
2 tbsp **agave nectar**
Pinch of **sea salt**

Combine the gin, sake, lime juice, cucumber, grapes, mint, agave nectar, and salt in a blender. Blend until frothy and smooth.

ORANGE WHISKEY SOUR

After a swig of this vitamin C-charged whiskey sour, you may agree with Lillian Carter, who claimed she liked "a little bourbon of an evening." We love to hunker down by the fire with this citrus-y bourbon blast. It's at its best when oranges are in season. Don't steer away because of the orange segments. If you are super-pressed for time, mandarin oranges make an acceptable substitute.

MAKES ABOUT 2 1/2 CUPS/600 ML; SERVES 2

1 cup/170 g **orange segments with their juice, chilled**
6 tbsp/90 ml **bourbon whiskey**
3 tbsp **agave nectar or turbinado sugar,**
    plus more to taste
2 tbsp **fresh lemon juice,** plus more to taste
2 cups/480 ml **ice cubes**

Combine the oranges and their juice and the bourbon in a blender. Add the 3 tbsp agave nectar, 2 tbsp lemon juice, and the ice. Blend until smooth. Taste and add more sugar or lemon juice, if you like.

watermeLon-RaSPBeRRy cooLie

This delightful blend of watermelon and strawberry is a jazzed-up riff on the classic strawberry daiquiri. The watermelon lightens the drink and adds freshness, while the raspberry sorbet gives it a sassy backdrop that pairs dynamically with the vodka. Because watermelon has an alkalinizing effect, it neutralizes the acidity of the booze and helps us in our ongoing quest to consume a more alkalinizing diet for good health. When time permits, we make our own ice cubes with the readily available electrolyte- or nutrient-enhanced waters for an extra boost of hydration, but feel free to experiment with any flavored ice cubes of your choice. Cranberry and goji berry juices work particularly well. Stay away from darker juices, which may taint the color of the drink.

MAKES ABOUT 2 1/2 CUPS/600 ML; SERVES 2

1 1/2 cups/220 g **diced seeded watermelon, chilled**
1/2 cup/55 g **frozen strawberries**
1/2 cup/115 g **raspberry sorbet**
1/3 cup/75 ml **light rum,** plus more to taste
1 tbsp **fresh lemon juice,** plus more to taste
2 tsp **agave nectar,** plus more to taste
Pinch of **sea salt**
4 to 6 **ice cubes**

Combine the watermelon and strawberries in a blender. Add the sorbet, 1/3 cup/75 ml rum, 1 tbsp lemon juice, 2 tsp agave nectar, salt, and ice. Blend until smooth. Taste and add more rum, lemon juice, and/or agave, if you like.

PINEAPPLE MOJITO SLUSH

This one is over the top! Freshly squeezed lime juice and mint is a winning combination, but it's the frozen pineapple that makes this mojito slush a standout. We used to serve this refreshing drink poolside, but when we learned how much vitamin C was in pineapple, we started to drink it during cold season as well. Now we have a crush on this slush all season long.

MAKES ABOUT 2 1/2 CUPS/600 ML; SERVES 2

1/2 cup/120 ml **club soda**
6 tbsp/90 ml **white rum**
12 medium **fresh mint leaves**
1/4 cup/60 ml **fresh lime juice,** plus more to taste
3 tbsp **agave nectar or sugar,** plus more to taste
1 1/2 cups/255 g **chopped frozen pineapple**
6 to 8 **ice cubes**

Combine the club soda, rum, mint, 1/4 cup/60 ml lime juice, and 3 tbsp agave nectar in a blender. Add the pineapple and ice. Blend until smooth. Taste and add more lime juice or agave nectar, if you like.

FACTOID: Bromelain, which is found in pineapples, has been found to help suppress coughs and loosen mucus.

POMEGRANATE COSMO

This icy pomegranate cocktail is an unexpected treat during the holiday season. It also makes a sensational autumnal dessert served fireside in a martini glass with a sugar rim and an orange-wheel garnish. Loaded with antioxidants and vitamin C, this holiday cheer is a gift to your taste buds and your immune system, too.

MAKES ABOUT 2 1/2 CUPS/600 ML; SERVES 2

3/4 cup/130 g **fresh red grapes, chilled**
1 1/4 cups/215 g **chopped frozen pineapple**
1 cup/240 ml **pomegranate-apple juice,
   made into ice cubes**
1/4 cup/60 ml **vodka**
2 tbsp **Grand Marnier**

Combine the grapes, pineapple, and pomegranate-apple ice cubes in a blender. Add the vodka and Grand Marnier. Blend until smooth.

Honeydew Gimlet

October and early November are celebrated months in California due to the greatly anticipated Indian summer. These months represent the height of honeydew season and the last of the autumnal poolside gatherings. Our guests rave about the unexpected combination of honeydew, grapes, and gin. Even our friends who are not lovers of gin can't believe the yum factor. Knowing that honeydew is a good source of vitamin C and potassium makes these gorgeous gimlets go down even easier.

MAKES ABOUT 2 1/2 CUPS/600 ML; SERVES 2

1 1/2 cups/255 g **frozen green grapes**
1 1/2 cups/255 g **frozen chopped honeydew melon**
6 tbsp/90 ml **gin**
1/4 cup/60 ml **fresh lime juice**
3 tbsp **agave nectar** OR **sugar**
3 **medium fresh basil leaves**
Pinch of **sea salt**

Combine the grapes and honeydew in a blender. Add the gin, lime juice, agave nectar, basil, and salt. Blend until smooth.

acai sangria

Because the word sangria means "bloody" in Portuguese and Spanish, it feels authentic to describe this acai smoothie sangria as bloody delicious and bloody healthful, too! Research indicates that moderate red-wine consumption may help protect against certain cancers and heart disease and can have a positive effect on blood pressure and cholesterol levels. When we are entertaining and want to go the extra mile for this recipe, we make Earl Grey tea ice cubes in place of regular ice cubes by steeping 3/4 cup/180 ml boiling filtered water with 2 tea bags and freezing. Acai Sangria tastes great with plain old ice, but the tea ice cubes do add superb dimension, and the caffeine will give your guests added zing. Plato may have been wiser than he knew when he said, "Nothing more excellent or valuable than wine was ever granted by the gods to man."

MAKES ABOUT 2 1/2 CUPS/600 ML; SERVES 2

3/4 cup/180 ml **fruity red wine, such as pinot noir**
Two 3 1/2-oz/100-g **frozen acai smoothie packs** OR
   3/4 cup/170 g **acai sorbet**
3/4 cup/85 g **frozen blueberries**
3/4 cup/85 g **frozen cherries**
2 tbsp **agave nectar**
1 tbsp **Grand Marnier**
1 tbsp **fresh lemon juice**
4 to 6 **ice cubes**

Combine the red wine, acai, blueberries, and cherries in a blender. Add the agave nectar, Grand Marnier, lemon juice, and ice. Blend until smooth.

BINDERS AND OTHER KEY INGREDIENTS

ACAI Grown in the Amazon rain forest, acai berries have a rich, berry-cocoa flavor. They contain more antioxidants than blueberries and pomegranates, plus omega fats, protein, and fiber—a combination that is said to boost energy, promote weight loss, and maintain healthy hearts, brains, and skin. Oprah Winfrey endorsed an acai product in 2008, and dozens of others have flooded the market, many in the form of pills. We consume acai, which is becoming more and more readily available in many markets, in various forms: acai nectar, acai sorbet by Häagen-Dazs, and Sambazon frozen acai smoothie packs, found in health-food stores. The smoothie packs come in original (sweetened) and unsweetened. All the recipes in this book are based on the original packs. We use the original smoothie packs in the morning and the sorbet in the afternoon for snacks or dessert. Alternatively, you can buy acai powder and acai nectar. Nectar, the undiluted juice of acai berries, pairs beautifully with blueberries. Our favorite brand is Bossa Nova.

AGAVE NECTAR Agave nectar (or syrup) is a fantastic natural sweetener that we can't live without. We use it in place of refined sugar as a healthier alternative. Because the taste of agave nectar is very mild, almost like simple syrup, it sweetens smoothies without tampering with the flavors of the fruit. A squirt or two can bring any smoothie alive, especially if the fruit is not at its peak. Agave nectar is sold in light, amber, dark, and raw varieties. We particularly like the blue agave nectar made from the *weber azul* for its neutral flavor and its low glycemic index, but feel free to experiment with the different types. The darker the color, the more caramel the nectar tastes. Raw agave is a perfect sweetener for raw foodists and the health conscious because it is produced at temperatures below 118°F/48°C to protect its natural enzymes. Agave nectar naturally contains quantities of iron, calcium, potassium, and magnesium, which contribute to the resulting color. Agave nectar is sweeter than sugar, so you need to use less.

ALMONDS Almonds produce an alkaline effect in the body. This means that alkaline, rather than acidic, substances are formed when you consume almonds. Soaking almonds for at least 4 hours or up to overnight can further enhance their alkaline properties and release enzyme inhibitors, making them easier to digest, so their nutrients are more easily absorbed. Strain and store them in the refrigerator for up to 3 days. We are big fans of raw almonds in smoothies, but almond butter makes a creamy substitute if desired.

ALMOND MILK We are fanatical about homemade nut milk. Though you can conveniently buy almond milk in tetra brick containers in supermarkets, once you make it yourself, you will never buy it again. We buy raw almonds when possible and store them in the freezer or refrigerator in an airtight container, as they quickly turn rancid at room temperature. We soak the almonds for at least 4 and up to 24 hours before blending them.

To make almond milk: Blend 3 cups/ 720 ml filtered water with 1 cup/115 g raw, soaked almonds in a high-speed blender at high speed for about 2 minutes. Season with 1 tsp vanilla extract/essence and a pinch of sea salt. For the most voluptuous almond milk, let the blended mixture sit for 15 to 20 minutes before straining the liquid through a fine-mesh sieve or clean cheesecloth.

BEE POLLEN Lauded in the Bible and ancient Chinese and Egyptian texts for its healing properties, bee pollen often has been called nature's most complete food. Alleged to stimulate organs and glands, enhance vitality, and lengthen life, bee pollen does noticeably increase energy levels, making it popular among athletes and others seeking a natural energy boost. Bee pollen adds a chalky texture to smoothies that some people like and others don't; Mary's not a fan, but Sara thinks it makes her Jasmine Honey Lassi (page 59) super-yummy.

BOBA Our kids love boba from their years of living in San Francisco, where boba tea (a.k.a. bubble tea) is readily available. Boba tea contains gelatinous tapioca balls called pearls, which are consumed through wide straws. The drink originated in Taiwan in the 1980s, spread to nearby East Asian countries, and migrated to Canada and then Chinatown in New York. When we moved out of San Francisco and didn't have the luxury of the Taiwanese drinks at hand, we started making them at home. Boba Tea Direct makes online ordering simple, and we really like the instant boba, which cooks up in about 5 minutes. Order the special fat straws for fun or have your kids eat the boba with a spoon.

BRAN Bran is the hard outer layer of cereal grains, such as oats, wheat, and rice. When the grains are harvested and processed, the outer layer is removed, creating the nutrient-rich by-product called bran. More nutritious than the processed grain, bran is extremely high in dietary fiber. It also makes a good protein source, delivers polyunsaturated and monounsaturated fats, and holds valuable vitamins and minerals. Simple bran is sometimes hard to find. Look for bran cereals that do not contain high-fructose corn syrup.

CACAO POWDER, CACAO NIBS, and COCOA POWDER When we first discovered cacao, we appreciated it more for the way it made us feel and for its health benefits—it's got tremendous ORAC value—than for its taste. Now we have grown so accustomed to the raw chocolate's pungent flavor (which is slightly bitter) that even bittersweet chocolate tastes a little too sweet and too rich. Cacao contains none of the butterfat that envelops the sweetened chocolate that you know and love. You would never want to eat cacao powder plain. Mix it with a smoothie or with milk to impart chocolate flavor. If you find cacao is too bitter or otherwise doesn't suit your fancy for smoothies, unsweetened cocoa powder is a good substitute.

If you like to nibble, try cacao nibs, little chunks of cacao. Initially we thought they resembled gravel on the tongue but soon found them yummy and addictive. Cacao nibs add a great crunchy texture to smoothies and give you a mega boost of energy and antioxidants.

Though cacao has recently stepped into the limelight, cocoa powder is tastier to many people and wonderful in smoothies. We prefer using unsweetened cocoa powder; Dutch-processed products are considered the best. Where cocoa's concerned, it's generally true that the more you pay, the better the quality. We generally opt for cocoa powder when we want a smooth finish without any bitter overtones.

CAMU CAMU This is a sour powder made from camu camu fruit, which is nothing short of a vitamin C bomb about the size of a small cherry. Camu camu fruit grows on trees rooted in the lush rain-forest soil of the Amazon River basin. The astonishing berry holds more vitamin C than any other known plant in the world. It has thirty times more vitamin C than an orange, ten times as much iron, three times the niacin, plus riboflavin, phosphorous, potassium, minerals, and amino acids. Claimed to have antiviral and antidepressant qualities, camu camu powder has replaced synthetic vitamin C for many people who say they find that it lifts their mood along with their energy, all while boosting the immune system. Camu camu powder can be ordered from Navitas Naturals (www.navitasnaturals.com).

CASHEWS We first started adding nuts to smoothies as a way of bolstering their protein content. Then we fell in love with the creaminess that they impart. Cashews, also known as "nature's vitamin pill," have been used to promote wellness for centuries, so we have embraced them in this new wave of smoothies. Packed with nutritional content, cashews have 5 grams of protein per ounce and high levels of the essential minerals iron, magnesium, phosphorus, zinc, copper, and manganese. Cashews do have a relatively high fat content (13 g per oz, 2 g saturated fat), but it is considered good fat. Surprisingly, cashew nuts contain less fat per serving than many other nuts, specifically almonds, walnuts, peanuts, and pecans. Despite the rich flavor of this nut, its oleic acid content promotes cardiovascular health. Like other nuts, cashews should be stored in the freezer or refrigerator in an airtight container, as they quickly turn rancid at room temperature. For a smoother smoothie, soak cashews in purified water for 6 to 8 hours, or overnight. Drain and rinse them before blending.

CHIA SEEDS Seeds of the chia plant, a relative of the mint family, were cultivated and eaten centuries ago by the Aztecs, Incans, and Mayans. *Chia* is the Mayan word for "strength," and these tiny, dark brown seeds live up to their name. They are making a major comeback today, thanks to their healthful omega oils, easily digestible protein, and antioxidants. Chia contains eight times more omega-3s than salmon, gram for gram. It is full of fiber, vitamins, and minerals, especially calcium and iron. It's a lot like flaxseed, but even better, as its natural antioxidants make chia's healthful fats more nutritionally stable. Research has shown chia to improve diabetes, hypoglycemia, celiac disease, and cholesterol. It produces a full feeling that's great for dieters, and slows the conversion of carbs to sugar, reducing ups and downs in blood sugar. Navitas Naturals offers chia seeds in their whole organic state and in a sprouted powder form. The powder can be sprinkled over granola or cereal, and serves beautifully as a super-healthful thickening agent for smoothies. Chia seeds also can be made into a gel that is easily digested and absorbed. We add this versatile gel to smoothies, milkshakes, hot or cold cereals, or yogurts. To make the gel, add 2 tbsp chia seeds to 1 cup/240 ml filtered water, stirring a few times with a whisk or fork. Store, tightly covered, in the refrigerator for up to 2 weeks.

CINNAMON You've probably known this warm, delicious spice all your life. You may not have known that cinnamon is tree bark. The spice is made by drying and grinding the brown bark of the cinnamon tree into powder, or using sticks of the dried bark for a gentle infusion. Cinnamon has a long history as both a food flavoring and medicine; cinnamon's healing abilities come from three components in the essential oils found in the bark, which exhibit anticlotting and antimicrobial effects and can help control blood sugar levels. Shake a little into your blender to spice up your smoothies.

COCONUT (Thai) Also referred to as a young coconut or a green coconut, this white husked coconut is not to be confused with the mature and familiar brown husked coconut. But a coconut by any name is so many things: milk, flesh, water, sugar, and oil, all in its own cup. Known as "the fluid of life," coconut water has the same electrolyte balance as human blood. It is more nutritious than whole milk and has less sugar than orange juice or sports drinks, and more potassium. Don't be daunted by the tough shell of a coconut; it really is easy to crack. The flesh varies in consistency; it may be thick and firm or thin and viscous. When selecting a coconut, avoid those with cracks, mold, and/or soft wet spots. You may not see them in the produce section of your supermarket, but they are readily available in Asian, Latino, and other ethnic or farmers' markets. Many health-food stores will carry them upon request.

To prepare coconut: Place the coconut on its side and shave the top portion of the white husk around the tip, using a cleaver or the bottom corner of a chef's knife. With the same corner of the knife, whack the exposed coconut shell approximately 1 in/2.5 cm inward from the outer edge, rotating the fruit in a circle until a "lid" is created. Pry the lid open and pour the coconut water into a blender. If there are shell pieces in the water, strain. Then use a metal spoon to scrape the inside of the coconut to remove the flesh. Clean off any bits of shell and add the flesh to the blender (the light brown skin that adheres to the flesh is palatable and okay to eat). Blend for 2 to 3 minutes at high speed until smooth. Because coconuts vary in size, and therefore the amount of water and flesh, the consistency of coconut milk varies considerably. As a rule of thumb, 1 part coconut flesh to 3 parts water works well for homemade coconut milk for smoothies. If the flesh or water is pinkish with gray overtones, it's rancid and should be discarded. See also COCONUT MILK

COCONUT BUTTER Unlike coconut oil, coconut butter is made from whole coconut flesh. It's made using a special blending process that transforms raw coconut into a buttery texture. The result is full of both coconut flavor and nutrition: oil, fiber, protein, vitamins, and minerals. Our favorite brand of coconut butter is Artisana; there are many online sites that sell it if you can't find it in local stores. The product is solid at room temperature, but soft and spreadable when warm. Put the jar in a bowl of warm water, then stir, and add to your blender. No refrigeration is necessary due to the stability of the healthful fatty acids within, but you'll find no trans fats here. We order coconut butter from www.premierorganics.org.

COCONUT MILK We love blending the water and meat of a Thai coconut to make our own coconut milk, but canned coconut milk makes a yummy substitute. Don't confuse coconut milk with sweetened "cream of coconut," which is loaded with sugar and artificial ingredients. Because canned coconut milk is thick and caloric, we like to dilute it with water, using 2 parts canned milk and 1 part water. Light coconut milk also works well in smoothies, though it is sometimes hard to find and is also pretty rich—if you are watching your waistline, use 2 parts light (often labeled "lite") coconut milk to 1 part water.

COCONUT OIL An edible oil that's been consumed in tropical places for thousands of years, coconut oil is said to prevent certain types of heart disease, increase immunity, aid digestion and metabolism, and even act as an antibacterial, antifungal agent that can fight some strains of candida yeast. Extra-virgin coconut oil maintains the flavor of coconut and refined coconut oil does not. When blended in a smoothie, splinters of the oil do not completely integrate. That's okay. We like it for the flavor, the added texture, and the health benefits.

COLD-BREW COFFEE We've only recently discovered and embraced cold-brew coffee. The cold process yields a brew with 70 percent less acidity than traditional coffee, and it tastes worlds smoother. Once you compare the two, you will become a convert! We think cold-brew coffee is at its best over ice and blended into smoothies. Read about the Toddy system at www.toddycafe.com, where you can learn how to make it at home or do what we do: order a gallon to have on hand when you are hankering for a Raspberry Cappuccino (page 83) or a Banana-Hazelnut Joe (page 17).

COTTAGE CHEESE This one may sound bizarre, but fear not. Blended into smoothies, cottage cheese is delicious. The cheese turns smoothies creamy and rich without an inordinate amount of fat. It's also low in carbohydrates but delivers a great dose of protein and calcium.

DHA (docosahexaenoic acid; children's) DHA is the omega-3 fatty acid that's received much publicity in recent years for its ability to enhance mental development, learning ability, and visual acuity. The brain and retina require large amounts of DHA and, while Americans generally consume enough of the plant-based fatty acid known as ALA, consumption of fish oil–based DHA is far below what is recommended. We like Nordic Naturals' supplement, which comes in a soft gel form. Smoothies are a perfect vehicle for getting this one into kids, as the drinks' bold fruit flavors mask the fishy flavor of DHA.

FLAXSEED and FLAXSEED OIL The earthy, nutty flavor of flaxseed, combined with an abundance of omega-3 fatty acids, has made them increasingly popular with healthy eaters. Slightly larger than sesame seeds with a hard, shiny shell, flaxseed can be eaten whole, ground to powder, or made into oil. True health fanatics prefer the seeds to the oil, but the oil delivers the same fatty acids that reduce inflammation, support bone health, and protect against heart disease, cancer, and diabetes. If you use flaxseed oil, make sure that you keep it refrigerated and adhere to the expiration dates. We like to buy whole flaxseed and grind it just before adding it to smoothies.

GELATIN We can't endorse Jell-O and other prepacked powdered gelatin dessert mixes on the market because they are filled with artificial ingredients. Alternatively, we highly suggest making your own, as they add fun and flair to smoothies for children. Following the directions on the back of the pack of unflavored gelatin, we like to use natural red juices such as pomegranate-apple or cherry because they give the best visual results. Always taste the prepared liquid gelatin before refrigerating it to see if you need to add a little sweetener, such as agave nectar, depending on your choice of fruit juice. Be careful not to overblend the jelled gelatin in the blender; just a pulse or two will yield squiggly results.

GINGER Aromatic, pungent, and spicy, ginger adds a unique flavor to any dish. Ground dried ginger is available in the spice section of supermarkets, but the fresh ginger, which absolutely explodes with flavor when grated or chopped, is also available year-round in the produce section. Aside from its inimitable flavor, ginger has a long history of alleviating gastrointestinal distress. It's a safe and effective way to relieve nausea during pregnancy. It also delivers anti-inflammatory and antioxidant effects and may protect against colorectal cancer. Ginger's tangy zing can really enliven a veggie smoothie or balance the sweetness of a fruity blend.

GOJI BERRIES A sweet red fruit native to Asia, goji berries have been used as a medicinal food for thousands of years. With more than 15 percent protein, 21 essential minerals, and 18 amino acids, goji berries promise myriad health benefits. They are known to strengthen immune systems, protect the liver, provide antiaging effects, build cardiovascular health, and improve vision. The flavor of goji berries lies somewhere between a cherry and cranberry but, as they're grainy in texture, they're not our favorite to eat by the handful. They work well in smoothies, pulverized into jam, or in a trail mix. We recommend using high-speed blenders. If you don't have one and you find goji berry seeds offensive, just strain them with a fine-mesh strainer.

GOLDEN BERRIES Also known as "Incan berries" or "cape gooseberries,"these sun-dried beauties taste like sweet-and-sour lemon candies and are packed with nutrition. They are a good source of protein, pectin, and vitamin P. Studies have shown that vitamin P, or bioflavinoids, possess antiviral, anticarcinogenic, anti-inflammatory, antihistamine, and antioxidant properties. Golden berries are seedy, so use a high-speed blender to incorporate them, or strain your smoothies with a fine-mesh strainer.

GRANOLA (sprouted live organic) We endorse sprouted live granola because it is raw and therefore the nutrients are not destroyed in the cooking process. Look for brands that are made from freshly sprouted, certified organically grown whole live grains, legumes, and seeds, with no flour. We believe that sprouting the grains is the most effective way to maximize nutrition. Most cereals on the market are overly processed and sprouted granola makes a great alternative.

HAZELNUTS We think hazelnuts are underrated. Originally known by the French name *filbert*, these flavorful nuts were later coined by the English as hazelnuts. Ancient Greek physicians and Chinese religious leaders sang the praises of hazelnuts; today, nutritionists hail them as a means to reduce the risk of cardiovascular disease, and as a

good source of vitamin E and magnesium. Of all tree nuts, hazelnuts have the highest proanthorcyanidin content, a compound known for adding an astringent flavor to foods and reducing the risk of blood clots and urinary tract infections. Store hazelnuts in the freezer or refrigerator in an airtight container, as they quickly turn rancid at room temperature.

HAZELNUT MILK In our opinion, hazelnuts make the fullest-flavored nut milk of all the nuts. Hazelnuts don't require soaking because they don't contain the enzyme inhibitors found in most nuts, so they make last-minute concoctions easy.

To make your own hazelnut milk: Blend 3 cups/720 ml filtered water with 1 cup/115 g raw hazelnuts in a high-speed blender for about 2 minutes. Season with 1 tsp vanilla extract/essence and a pinch of sea salt. For the most voluptuous hazelnut milk, let the blended mixture sit for 15 to 20 minutes before straining out the blended nuts in a sieve or clean cheesecloth.

HEMP SEEDS Though just a little seed, hemp is one of the highest sources of complete protein of all plant-based foods. Hemp seeds contain all of the essential amino acids, they are highly digestible, and offer a well-balanced ratio of fatty acids, which are excellent for cardiovascular health and promote a strong immune system. Also a good source of fiber, magnesium, iron, zinc, and potassium, hemp seeds work well in smoothies, or can be sprinkled on granola, yogurt, or salads. Look for them at health food stores, or order online from Navitas Naturals.

HONEY Honey, that oft-called "nectar of the gods" actually produced by mortal, hard-working bees and derived from flower nectar, is a mixture of sugar (mainly fructose and glucose) and other compounds. The specific makeup of any batch of honey will depend on the mix of flowers available to the bees that made it. There are several types of honey on the market. Raw honey remains as it exists in the hive, unheated and unprocessed. Although it is sometimes strained, it may contain some pollen and small bits of wax. Strained honey generally is raw and, while large particles are extracted through straining, it may have a cloudy appearance because of the pollen still within it. Ultrafiltered honey, which is heated and filtered under high pressure, is preferred by supermarkets because it crystallizes more slowly and thus has a longer shelf life. We prefer raw honey, as it maintains nutritionally valuable enzymes.

IRISH MOSS Irish moss is a species of red algae often used in living foods cuisine. Collected from the rocky Atlantic coastlines of Europe and North America, Irish moss, or carrageen moss, is a good substitute for animal-derived gelatin. It can be used to thicken puddings, pies, ice cream, and smoothies. Used medicinally for centuries, Irish moss is rich in iodine and sulfur. It contains beta-carotene, calcium, iron, magnesium, manganese, phosphorous, selenium, zinc, gel-forming polysaccharides (known as carrageenans), pectin, B vitamins, and vitamin C. Said to reduce inflammation, Irish moss can aid respiratory problems and soothe coughs and sore throats. It helps with digestion and thyroid function and aids weight loss by delivering a sense of fullness as it's digested.

To prepare Irish moss: Working with small amounts at a time, rinse thoroughly under cold running water, using your fingertips to remove any sand or small plastic threads left over from harvesting. Place up to the amount you think you may use in a week in an airtight container and add cold water, preferably filtered, to cover. Cover tightly and let soak in the refrigerator for at least 24 hours and up to 1 week. (The moss is most effective after 24 hours and begins losing its ability to congeal over time.) Drain thoroughly before using as directed in recipes.

For an easy way to use Irish moss medicinally, gelatinize it by blending 1/2 cup/30 g of soaked moss with 1 1/2 cups/ 360 ml filtered water. Blend in a high-speed blender until moss is completely broken down. You can keep this in your refrigerator for up to 2 weeks. Add 2 to 3 tbsp (or more) to juices or smoothies and blend well before drinking. Irish moss can be ordered at www.cafegratitude.com or www.purejoyplanet.com. Refrigerate as soon as you receive it.

KEFIR Think of kefir as a drinkable yogurt that contains different types of beneficial bacteria. Both kefir and yogurt are cultured milk products. Yogurt contains beneficial bacteria that pass through the digestive track, keeping it clean and providing food for the friendly bacteria that reside there. But kefir goes a step further, by actually colonizing the intestinal tract. If you aren't accustomed to plain kefir, we recommend that you start with one that is flavored. Kefir comes in all sorts of flavors from peach and raspberry to vanilla and blackberry. Plain kefir has less sugar, but sometimes has a musky flavor that can be offensive to some. *See also* YOGURT

KOMBUCHA Celebrated in China for thousands of years, kombucha is a sweet and sour, fermented, slightly carbonated drink. Historic Chinese lore claims kombucha to be a "fountain of youth elixir" that holds a mystical element of alchemy and magic. This unique tea was used during sacred rites and attracted many who were in search of health and longevity. Suddenly available even at American convenience stores, kombucha has myriad modern health claims, from lengthening life to thickening hair, lowering blood pressure and cholesterol, and improving menopausal symptoms. Its vinegary taste takes a little getting used to. If you are a novice, acquaint yourself with one of the many flavored kombuchas (grape, cranberry, ginger, guava) before drinking the plain kombuchas.

MANGOSTEEN Unrelated to mangos, mangosteens are dark purple fruits about the size of a small peach. Grown in the hot, humid climates of southeast Asia, mangosteen rinds have been used medicinally for generations. Instead of peeling the rind, open the fruit by pressing firmly or twisting until it breaks apart. Inside is a soft, opaque, white flesh, which looks like a head of garlic, but tastes sweet and tart. In North America, fresh mangosteens can be found in Canada and Hawaii, but cannot be imported to the continental United States because of concerns that they transport insects. In 2002, however, a Utah-based company introduced a mangosteen drink called XanGo, and another superfruit craze was born. Note that some mangosteen nectars are more concentrated than others, so add it in small doses and taste as you go.

MAPLE SYRUP Good old maple syrup is a fantastic natural sweetener that is far healthier than refined sugar and contains fewer calories and a higher concentration of minerals than honey. An excellent source of manganese and a good source of zinc, maple syrup is good for your heart and sweet to your immune system. To make maple syrup, maple trees are tapped for sap. The sap is then boiled to evaporate the water content, leaving behind syrup of varying grades. We like the light amber syrup for its mild flavor, but feel free to follow your own tastes.

MATCHA POWDER One of the most common green teas out there, matcha is different in that the bright green leaves are not strained or left in the pot; instead, they are ground to a powder and consumed. Because of this, brewed matcha contains higher concentrations of vitamins and anti-

oxidants than most other teas. It contains the powerful antioxidant EGCG (epigallocatechin gallate), which can modulate metabolism to promote weight control, and the amino acid, theanine, which helps regulate moods. Matcha also claims powerful antiaging effects, an ability to lower blood pressure, fight cancer, ease constipation, and stabilize blood sugar levels. It is a strong detoxifier and alkalizer due to its high chlorophyll content. Matcha is fine to sip plain, but it also makes a great addition to smoothies, as it has less caffeine than coffee and delivers a major energy boost without the jitters.

MILK With lots of protein and calcium, milk is a great way to achieve a creamy, delicious smoothie. We do, however, have a few caveats in the milk department. First, we highly recommend using raw milk if you can get your hands on it (it's only sold commercially in a few states and otherwise is available only from local dairies). Pasteurization can destroy lactic acid–producing bacteria in milk that protect against pathogens. The heat used in the process alters milk's amino acids, and it promotes rancidity of unsaturated fatty acids and destruction of vitamins. Furthermore, pasteurization destroys all the enzymes in milk, which help the body assimilate body-building elements such as calcium. If you can't find raw milk, be sure to buy organic milk enhanced with DHA. One of the omega-3 fatty acids, DHA is required in the brain and retina and is essential to learning ability, mental development, and visual acuity. It's an important nutrient for pregnant women, children, and all adults, and Americans' current intake of DHA is alarmingly low. Last, with so many of us spending too much time indoors and diligently using sunscreen when we're out, deficiency in vitamin D, which can be absorbed from sunlight, is on the rise. You can remedy the shortfall by consuming foods containing vitamin D, such as milk.

MILK POWDER Nonfat dry milk offers a great way to add creaminess to smoothies with less fat and less liquid. When you want a creamy smoothie but don't want to add a cup of milk, use a few tablespoons of the powdered variety to make it rich and yummy.

OATS Eating oats is a great way to lower your cholesterol. Antioxidants unique to this grain help cut the risk of cardiovascular disease and, unlike other grains, oats typically retain their bran when harvested, making them a great source of fiber. Do stay away from instant or quick-cooking oats as they are highly processed. Steel-cut oats don't incorporate well in smoothies; old-fashioned rolled oats work best. If time permits, there are health benefits to soaking oats in water for at least 6 hours, or up to overnight. This process neutralizes the phytic acid and the enzyme inhibitors, making the oats more digestible and bioavailable. Drain and rinse with filtered water before adding them to smoothies as a healthful, tasty thickener.

OLIVE OIL (EXTRA-VIRGIN) The key to healthful Mediterranean diets for centuries, olive oil is the only vegetable oil that can be consumed in its natural state, freshly pressed from the fruit. The high amounts of monounsaturated fatty acids and antioxidants found in olive oil deliver considerable health benefits, chief among them protection against heart disease. Add the tastiest olive oil that you have in your pantry to smoothies. We like a mild yet flavorful blend that isn't too green. Make sure your olive oil is fresh and has been stored properly in a cool, dark place for the best smoothies.

PEANUTS and PEANUT BUTTER
Filling, sweet, and savory, peanut butter is a great means to a hearty smoothie with unparalleled creaminess. In addition to their high monounsaturated fat content, peanuts feature an array of other nutrients that have been shown to promote heart health in numerous studies. Peanuts are a good source of vitamin E, niacin, folate, protein, and manganese. Many traditional peanut butters are loaded with excess sugar, sodium, and other junk, so be sure to read the labels. We are adamant about purchasing organic peanut butter to avoid the harmful chemicals and pesticides used in some commercial production. Look for our favorite brand, Justin's Nut Butter, out of Boulder, Colorado.

PECANS Pecans add a really nice twist to smoothies. Their distinct flavor pairs especially well with oranges and cranberries, as well as with blueberries. On top of adding a subtle sweetness, pecans deliver a good dose of protein and unsaturated fats. The antioxidants and plant sterols in these nuts can reduce high cholesterol. One study found, in fact, that eating about a handful of pecans each day may help lower cholesterol levels as much as cholesterol-lowering medications. Store pecans in the freezer or refrigerator in an airtight container, as they quickly turn rancid at room temperature.

POMEGRANATE In the Greek myth of Persephone, the pomegranate is called "the fruit of the underworld," yet in the Muslim Qur'an it is called "the fruit of paradise." Though the ancients used pomegranate skin and bark for medicinal purposes, only the seeds are edible. Sweet, tart, and juicy, the seeds, or arils, are low in calories, high in vitamin C and potassium, and a good source of fiber. Pomegranate juice is high in three different types of polyphenols, which is a potent form of antioxidants. Fresh pomegranate is available from September until January. We do not add pomegranate seeds to smoothies, as they are too seedy, but pomegranate juice (from concentrate) is readily available. Experiment with the wide range of brands on the market. Some juices are very tart and concentrated; others mix pomegranate juice with blueberry or apple to round out the flavor.

PROBIOTICS Probiotics have powered into the health arena with great gusto. Known as "good" bacteria, probiotics occur naturally in certain yogurts and fermented dairy drinks, such as kefir. They are added to certain foods and are also found in supplement form. Probiotics have been used as a treatment for a variety of gastrointestinal diseases including irritable bowel, lactose intolerance, traveler's diarrhea, and antibiotic-induced diarrhea. By consuming probiotic foods, we can increase the number of healthful bacteria, boost our immunity, and promote healthy digestive systems.

PUMPKIN SEEDS Roasted pumpkin seeds are subtly sweet and nutty in flavor and just may be one of the most nutritious seeds around. Just-out-of-the-pumpkin seeds are encased in yellowish husks, but when purchased raw or roasted, they appear dark green and flat. A rich source of minerals, protein, and monounsaturated fats, pumpkin seeds may protect men from prostate cancer, lower cholesterol, and reduce arthritis-related inflammation.

RED WINE A surefire way to enliven a smoothie and your guests, red wine makes a superb addition to cocktail smoothies. It isn't all about indulgence, either; red wine contains resveratrol, the phenolic antioxidant also found in red grapes that exhibits anticancer, anti-inflammatory, and beneficial cardiovascular effects.

RICE MILK A good alternative to cow's milk if anyone in your family is lactose-intolerant or vegan, rice milk is usually processed from brown rice and is unsweetened. It contains more carbohydrates than cow's milk, but no significant calcium or protein, so buy a commercial brand that's fortified with vitamins and minerals.

SEA SALT It may sound counterintuitive to add a pinch of salt to certain smoothies, but it heightens flavor, especially in recipes that feature melons. We particularly love Himalayan sea salt. Said to be the purest salt on Earth and uncontaminated with toxins or pollutants, Himalayan crystal salt retains trace minerals that table and cooking salts lack. Because of this salt's makeup, it is difficult for the body to absorb too much, so it does not contribute to high blood pressure the way typical table salt can. Supporters claim Himalayan sea salt helps regulate water content in the body as well as blood sugar, along with a host of other benefits.

SOFT SILKEN TOFU This may sound unappealing but, trust us, it's not! Soft silken tofu adds a creamy texture to smoothies and has great health benefits. It is low in calories for the protein it packs; it's cholesterol free and provides a good source of calcium and iron. With a softer consistency than regular tofu, silken tofu is sometimes packaged in aseptic boxes that don't require refrigeration, so you may find it in a different section of the grocery store than regular tofu. Soft silken tofu is especially good with strong flavors that mask its distinct taste, such as pineapple, banana, peanut butter, and cocoa powder.

SORBETS The good news about sorbet is that it is fat free. The bad news is that many commercial sorbets are full of refined sugars, as well as natural sugars. Consequently, we consider smoothies made with sorbets to be on the decadent side. They make great desserts, which may seldom be the healthiest course but is always beloved and can be had with little to no guilt. For the smoothie recipes in this book, look for passion-fruit, coconut, chocolate, tangerine, raspberry, açaí, and pomegranate sorbets, preferably organic products that do not use high-fructose corn syrup or artificial flavors.

SOY FROZEN YOGURT Soy frozen yogurt makes a great nondairy binder for smoothies and a lactose-free treat for those who want to stay away from ice cream. It adds a rich creaminess to smoothies, and its yogurt status comes with those gut-friendly live active cultures. With flavors like vanilla bean and crème caramel out now, this is a must-try for smoothie enthusiasts. We always buy organic soy products if available.

SOY MILK Produced by soaking dry soybeans and grinding them with water, soy milk is a great source of protein and isoflavones. Isoflavones are phytochemicals which are being studied in relation to the relief of certain menopausal symptoms, cancer prevention, slowing or reversing osteoporosis, and reducing the risk of heart disease. Lactose free and nondairy, soy milk makes a good substitute for cow's milk in smoothies or cereal, or by the glass. Note that flavored soy milk, such as vanilla and chocolate, has the addition of evaporated cane juice. Plain soy milk does not.

SUNFLOWER SEEDS The little gray seeds of the beautiful sunflower make a great snack and a superb shot of nutrition in smoothies. A main source of polyunsaturated oil, sunflower seeds supply significant amounts of vitamin E. The anti-inflammatory effects of vitamin E reduce symptoms of asthma, osteoarthritis, and rheumatoid arthritis. These tiny seeds also deliver a large dose of magnesium, which, studies have shown, helps prevent migraine headaches, lower high blood pressure, and reduce the risk of heart attack and stroke.

TEAS So many wonderful and wildly different teas abound. Here we mention a few of our favorites for smoothies. We brew them to double strength to enhance the flavor profile and reap their health benefits. Be careful not to oversteep, however, as the tea will turn out bitter. In some recipes, we suggest the added step of freezing tea into ice cubes.

Chai tea is the East's answer to the morning cup of coffee. This Indian black tea is brewed strong, with a combination of spices that vary from recipe to recipe but usually consist of cinnamon, cardamom, cloves, pepper, and ginger. Every ingredient in chai tea is good for you, and when you put them all together they pack a powerful punch for your immune system.

Earl Grey tea has long been consumed for its antioxidant properties, but its key ingredient, bergamot, helps relieve the symptoms of anxiety and depression.

Jasmine is our favorite green tea because of its delicate floral essence. It's a superb little energy boost without a sharp, acidic flavor.

Peppermint tea's active ingredient is the essential oil, menthol, which is refreshing to drink, but also known to promote digestion, relieve stomach aches, and prevent gallstones. It is also used to ease headaches and colic in babies.

Raspberry-leaf tea is caffeine free. The brand we prefer, Traditional Medicinals, can be found at natural-foods stores.

Thai tea is hard to find at supermarkets but is available at Asian markets or can be ordered from www.bobateadirect.com. We've found that Thai tea is best when made with loose tea leaves, as opposed to tea bags. Bright orange and super-sweet, it's often made with condensed milk and half-and-half/half cream and served cold over ice.

Yerba maté is an acquired taste that we have come to like. A traditional South American infusion with an herbal grassy essence, its smoky tobacco flavor can be off-putting, but, when paired with fruits, its flavor blends nicely. Full of nutrition, yerba maté gives you an alert, energized feeling without the jitters associated with caffeine.

VANILLA (Vanilla Extract/essence, Vanilla Water, Vanilla Bean)

The vanilla bean, or pod, comes from the only edible fruit–bearing orchid in the world.

We think vanilla is the world's finest flavor, one that adds an aromatic flavor profile and depth to smoothies. Vanilla extract (called vanilla essence in some regions) is a great way to get that flavor into your smoothies—we recommend the heavenly Madagascar Bourbon Vanilla—but it's not the freshest or purest way. Liquid vanilla, the raw version of extract, is a vanilla concentrate like no other. To make it, we chop four whole vanilla beans into 1/2-in/12-mm pieces and combine them in a high-speed blender with 1 cup/240 ml purified water. Blend on high until no chunks remain. The result is pure vanilla essence with no alcohol. It will keep in the refrigerator for up to 3 months, or you can freeze it. If you have a high-speed blender but not a lot of time, just cut a 1-in/2.5-cm piece of vanilla bean and hurl it into the blender along with the fruit and binder. If you don't have a high-speed blender or don't care to make vanilla water but like the idea of the fresh bean, just cut open the pod lengthwise and scrape the tiny black seeds into your blender for a sublime fresh taste. We order our vanilla beans from www.penzys.com.

WHEY PROTEIN POWDER A high-quality protein derived from cow's milk, whey is both highly nutritious and more soluble than other proteins. It contains essential amino acids that are the building blocks of muscle tissue, skin, nails, and bones. Supplements can be found in powder form and purport to benefit weight management, cardiovascular health, infant nutrition, and healthy aging, while working against cancer and diabetes. Soy protein offers a similar amino-acid boost for people who want to stay away from dairy.

YACON SYRUP and POWDER
Nicknamed "the apple of the earth" due to its sweet, juicy crunch, yacon is a tuber that can be eaten fresh but, more commonly, is made into syrup or powder to serve as a natural sugar substitute. With a flavor similar to molasses, yacon has high levels of inulin, a complex sugar that is not digestible and simply passes through the body, leaving yacon with about half the calories of average sugar sources. The substance also promotes the production of probiotics, or healthful bacteria, which can contribute to better digestion and colon health. Navitas Naturals offers yacon in both syrup and powder forms.

YOGURT This ingredient does wonders for smoothies. Yogurt adds creaminess, flavor, protein, calcium, and, perhaps most important, live active cultures that keep your digestive system (and others) on track. Look for probiotic beverages such as Activia, which contain healthful bacteria (renamed and trademarked for marketing reasons as Bifidus Regularis), and Greek yogurt as alternatives to conventional varieties. Greek yogurt is creamier than regular yogurt as it is strained in a centuries-old process that removes the whey, or liquid, from the yogurt. In addition to outstanding creaminess, the process also leaves Greek yogurt higher in protein and lower in lactose than regular yogurt. *See also* KEFIR

NUTRITIONAL INFORMATION

The "bonuses" in the last column identify further bragging rights for individual smoothies, such as particularly good to high amounts of vitamins, amino acids, antioxidants, and other substances, some given in the percentage of Daily Value (DV) or Daily Reference Value (DRV).

	CALORIES	PROTEIN (g)	CARBOHYDRATE (g)	FIBER (g)	TOTAL FAT (g)
CASHEW BLUE	329	6	51	4	13
CACAO FRENZY	334	9	43	5	15
PEACH PIE MATÉ	194	5	44	3	1
BANANA-HAZELNUT JOE	280	7	38	4	12
GREEN ENERGY	246	4	40	5	10
THAI BUBBLE TEA SLUSH	381	3	81	4	5
KOMBUCHA, BABY!	126	1	31	5	1
POMEGRANATE MOCHA	242	5	50	3	2
CHA CHA CHAI	133	2	34	3	0
SUPER C	180	4	46	5	1
HAPPY HEART	229	4	54	9	2
HUSH THE HORMONES	199	3	46	3	2
NO MORE NAUSEA	223	5	51	4	1
CANCER KICKER	195	5	22	6	12
PREGO MAMA	293	3	73	4	1
BLUEBERRY BRAIN BOOST	281	4	51	9	10

SATURATED FAT (g)	MONO- AND POLYUNSATURATED FATS (g)	CHOLESTEROL (mg)	SODIUM (mg)	NUTRITION BONUS
2	11	0	13	–
4	11	15	62	calcium 24% DV
21	0	4	48	vitamin C 321% DV, chromium 87% DV
1	11	4	92	calcium 25% DV
1	9	0	45	33 mg antioxidant EGCG
3	2	18	133	–
2	11	0	13	50 mg antioxidant EGCG
0	2	0	59	vitamin C 51% DV
0	0	0	5	vitamin C 64% DV
0	0	0	9	vitamin C 144% DV
0	2	0	28	fiber 36% DRV, vitamin C 107% DV
0	2	0	17	vitamin C 75% DV, calcium 17% DV
1	0	3	52	vitamin C 303% DV, calcium 15% DV
2	10	2	814	16 mg lycopene, vitamin C 81% DV, folate 30% DV
0	0	0	79	vitamin C 121% DV, folate 16% DV
1	9	0	7	1 g omega-3s

	CALORIES	PROTEIN (g)	CARBOHYDRATE (g)	FIBER (g)	TOTAL FAT (g)
ADIOS, ARTHRITIS	271	7	50	2	3
PRETTY 'N' PINK	153	1	39	4	1
POM ACAI	219	2	52	5	4
GOJI GREATNESS	221	4	52	4	0
COCONUT AMBROSIA	237	6	36	8	9
AVO-COLADA	231	3	46	6	6
BETA-CAROTENE BLAST	237	3	60	5	1
CRAN-TASTIC	253	1	65	6	1
GAZPACHO GRATITUDE	119	3	18	4	5
STRAWBERRIES all the WHEY	255	12	48	3	3
RASPBERRY RITUAL	214	9	43	7	3
APPLE-FLAX FRAPPÉ	351	12	48	9	15
JASMINE HONEY LASSI	249	9	55	3	2
PURPLE HAZE	305	10	45	4	11
FIBER 5	314	8	51	6	13
APPLE, CUKE, PARSLEY, MINT	223	9	33	7	8
PINEAPPLE, ARUGULA, MACADAMIA NUT	269	5	40	9	12

SATURATED FAT (g)	MONO- AND POLYUNSATURATED FATS (G)	CHOLESTEROL (MG)	SODIUM (MG)	NUTRITION BONUS
2	1	10	83	vitamin C 57% DV, calcium 17% DV
0	0	0	6	–
0	4	0	17	–
0	4	0	90	vitamin C 104% DV
1	8	0	268	fiber 32% DRV, potassium 25% DV, vitamin C 81% DV
1	5	0	241	potassium 21% DV
0	0	0	21	vitamin C 278% DV
0	0	0	9	fiber 24% DRV
1	4	0	621	10 mg lycopene, vitamin C 106% DV
2	1	10	184	calcium 35% DV, vitamin C 117% DV, iron 25% DV
1	2	8	188	fiber 28% DRV, calcium 16% DV
2	13	4	60	2 g omega-3s, fiber 36% DRV, calcium 20% DV
1	1	6	3	vitamin C 296% DV
2	9	6	83	calcium 25% DV, vitamin C 55% DV
2	11	6	48	2 g omega-3s, folate 20% DV, calcium 18% DV
1	7	0	45	2 g omega-3s, iron 55% DV
1	11	0	112	3 g omega-3s, fiber 36% DRV

	CALORIES	PROTEIN (g)	CARBOHYDRATE (g)	FIBER (g)	TOTAL FAT (g)
KALE, APPLE, CARROT	249	5	34	5	12
PERSIMMON, CRANBERRY, SPINACH	133	1	34	5	0
ORANGE, SUGAR SNAP PEA, PUMPKIN SEED	284	8	36	9	13
CARROT, BEET, WATERCRESS	184	4	29	4	8
TOMATO, RED PEPPER, PARSLEY, LIME	200	4	20	4	13
ACAI COLADA	341	1	83	4	2
SWEET 'N' SALTY PEANUT CRUNCH	562	21	43	8	37
PASSION BERRY BLISS	225	4	53	6	1
COCONUT DREAM CREAM	235	3	41	6	8
NAKED ANGEL ICED TEA	166	1	43	2	0
RASPBERRY CAPPUCCINO	304	6	65	9	4
WATERMELON AGUA FRESCA	96	2	25	3	0
PINEAPPLE PIZZAZZ	177	2	45	6	1
ELECTROLYTE ELIXIR	115	1	29	2	0
MUCHO MATCHA	269	7	56	2	3
MELON MOJO	147	2	37	4	1
BLUEBERRY-ACAI MOUSSE	191	2	43	3	3
SKINNY ME	145	2	29	4	0

SATURATED FAT (g)	MONO- AND POLYUNSATURATED FATS (G)	CHOLESTEROL (MG)	SODIUM (MG)	NUTRITION BONUS
1	11	0	76	4 g omega 3s, potassium 25% DV, vitamin E 23% DV
0	0	0	24	vitamin A 33% DV
2	11	0	11	3 g omega-3s, fiber 36% DRV, iron 25% DV
1	7	0	86	2 g omega-3s
1	12	0	349	4 mg lycopene, potassium 22% DV
2	0	0	37	Iron 22% DV, vitamin C 53% DV
6	31	3	272	protein 42% DRV, fiber 32% DRV, potassium 23% DV
1	0	3	35	vitamin C 103% DV
6	2	0	301	potassium 22% DV
0	0	0	12	vitamin A 48% DV, vitamin C 98% DV
2	2	12	91	fiber 36% DRV, calcium 22% DV, vitamin C 141% DV
0	0	0	81	10 mg lycopene, vitamin C 88% DV
0	0	0	11	vitamin C 193% DV
0	0	0	122	5 mg lycopene
1	2	6	96	66 mg antioxidant EGCG, calcium 26% DV, vitamin C 86% DV
0	0	0	112	vitamin C 193% DV, vitamin K 59% DV, potassium 22% DV
2	3	0	80	-
0	0	0	2	vitamin C 154% DV

	CALORIES	PROTEIN (g)	CARBOHYDRATE (g)	FIBER (g)	TOTAL FAT (g)
GREEK GODDESS	151	13	21	3	3
ORANGE JULIA	244	12	50	3	0
SMARTY PANTS	258	5	54	4	4
PEANUT BANANA FOFANA	434	17	41	6	25
SASSY STRAWBERRY GRANOLA CRUNCH	275	8	54	5	5
PINK-A-LICIOUS	323	7	50	7	13
GOODNESS GRAPENESS	209	2	53	2	0
NECTARINE-Y	141	3	35	4	1
BANANA BUBBLE	168	7	31	2	2
WATERMELON JIGGLY	197	2	49	2	0
CUCUMBER SAKE-TINI	370	1	27	2	0
ORANGE WHISKEY SOUR	220	1	30	2	0
WATERMELON-RASPBERRY COOLIE	180	2	21	1	0
PINEAPPLE MOJITO SLUSH	235	1	37	2	0
POMEGRANATE COSMO	267	1	45	2	0
HONEYDEW GIMLET	326	2	55	3	1
ACAI SANGRIA	175	1	23	3	1

SATURATED FAT (g)	MONO- AND POLYUNSATURATED FATS (G)	CHOLESTEROL (MG)	SODIUM (MG)	NUTRITION BONUS
2	1	9	506	-
0	0	6	178	calcium 39% DV, iron 17% DV, vitamin C 150% DV
1	3	12	53	1 g omega-3s, vitamin C 65% DV, calcium 16% DV
5	20	0	47	protein 34% DRV, potassium 26% DV, calcium 15% DV
1	3	5	96	vitamin C 75% DV, calcium 19% DV
2	11	0	10	fiber 28% DRV, vitamin C 80% DV, iron 17% DV
0	0	0	39	vitamin C 83% DV
0	0	0	0	-
1	1	6	90	calcium 25% DV
0	0	0	130	5 mg lycopene, vitamin C 94% DV
0	0	0	84	-
0	0	0	130	vitamin C 91% DV
0	0	0	25	5 mg lycopene, vitamin C 45% DV
0	0	0	22	vitamin C 114% DV
0	0	0	10	vitamin C 152% DV
0	0	0	141	potassium 23% DV, vitamin C 54% DV
0	0	0	1	-

INDEX